Editor-in-Chief and Founder:
  Lyndon H. LaRouche, Jr.
Editorial Board: *Lyndon H. LaRouche, Jr. , Helga
  Zepp-LaRouche, Robert Ingraham, Tony
  Papert, Gerald Rose, Dennis Small, Jeffrey
  Steinberg, William Wertz*
Co-Editors: *Robert Ingraham, Tony Papert*
Managing Editor: *Nancy Spannaus*
Technology: *Marsha Freeman*
Books: *Katherine Notley*
Ebooks: *Richard Burden*
Graphics: *Alan Yue*
Photos: *Stuart Lewis*
Circulation Manager: *Stanley Ezrol*

INTELLIGENCE DIRECTORS
Counterintelligence: *Jeffrey Steinberg, Michele
  Steinberg*
Economics: *John Hoefle, Marcia Merry Baker,
  Paul Gallagher*
History: *Anton Chaitkin*
Ibero-America: *Dennis Small*
Russia and Eastern Europe: *Rachel Douglas*
United States: *Debra Freeman*

INTERNATIONAL BUREAUS
Bogotá: *Miriam Redondo*
Berlin: *Rainer Apel*
Copenhagen: *Tom Gillesberg*
Houston: *Harley Schlanger*
Lima: *Sara Madueño*
Melbourne: *Robert Barwick*
Mexico City: *Gerardo Castilleja Chávez*
New Delhi: *Ramtanu Maitra*
Paris: *Christine Bierre*
Stockholm: *Ulf Sandmark*
United Nations, N.Y.C.: *Leni Rubinstein*
Washington, D.C.: *William Jones*
Wiesbaden: *Göran Haglund*

ON THE WEB
e-mail: eirns@larouchepub.com
www.larouchepub.com
www.executiveintelligencereview.com
www.larouchepub.com/eiw
Webmaster: *John Sigerson*
Assistant Webmaster: *George Hollis*
Editor, Arabic-language edition: *Hussein Askary*

EIR (ISSN 0273-6314) *is published weekly
(50 issues), by EIR News Service, Inc.,
P.O. Box 17390, Washington, D.C. 20041-0390.
(703) 777-9451*

European Headquarters: E.I.R. GmbH, Postfach
Bahnstrasse 9a, D-65205, Wiesbaden, Germany
Tel: 49-611-73650
Homepage: http://www.eirna.com
e-mail: eirna@eirna.com
Director: Georg Neudecker

Montreal, Canada: 514-461-1557

Denmark: EIR - Danmark, Sankt Knuds Vej 11,
basement left, DK-1903 Frederiksberg, Denmark.
Tel.: +45 35 43 60 40, Fax: +45 35 43 87 57. e-mail:
eirdk@hotmail.com.

Mexico City: EIR, Sor Juana Inés de la Cruz 242-2
Col. Agricultura C.P. 11360
Delegación M. Hidalgo, México D.F.
Tel. (5525) 5318-2301
eirmexico@gmail.com

Canada Post Publication Sales Agreement
#40683579

Postmaster: Send all address changes to *EIR*, P.O.
Box 17390, Washington, D.C. 20041-0390.

Signed articles in *EIR* represent the views of the
authors, and not necessarily those of the Editorial
Board.

What We Do Now
Is Crucial

Bust the British Empire and Go With the Eurasia Solution

Feb. 21—Lyndon LaRouche today delivered a strategic assessment that the world has reached a turning-point moment, such that either the power of the evil British empire, with its system of monetarist looting, is crushed, or the world will soon plunge into the horrors of thermonuclear war. While there is legitimate focus on the insane provocations coming out of Turkey and Saudi Arabia, who are attempting to do everything possible to start World War III on the Syria-Turkey border, the reality is that the real seat of power behind these maneuvers is the British Crown.

The trans-Atlantic British system is totally bankrupt, and the real center of global power and stability has shifted to Asia, where collaboration between China, Russia, and India has created a relative stability, by trans-Atlantic standards. There are threats in Asia, but these threats can be defeated by the kind of physical economic development policies that China has advanced with the One Belt One Road initiative. Asia has become the center of humanity's future because the British have destroyed almost every ounce of creativity in the United States, Britain, and much of continental Europe. There are options, but they all begin with the wiping out of the power of the British Empire.

For continental Europe, the only productive solution is for Germany, the last remaining economic force in Europe, to align with Russia around a plan for physical economic development, across the entire corridor between Germany and Russia. A Russia-Germany coalition for a revival of the productive forces would be the kind of change, away from British Empire monetarism, that is urgently needed. Forget the bankrupt system of British empire money. It is all gone and can never be revived. A German alignment with Russia to build the productive links across Eurasia, in partnership with China and India, spells doom for the forces of empire that are driving for war, using pawns like Erdogan, Obama, and Mohammed bin Salman.

The same approach is urgently required in Northeast Asia, where the Korea crisis can only be solved by a revival of the China-Korea-Russia rail links that have historically existed and can and must be revived today. Without a physical economic dimension, there is no way to defeat the British geopolitical swindles. The late Gen. Douglas MacArthur understood this principle of Asia development and stability, as seen by his program for rebuilding Japan at the close of World War II and his brilliant leadership in Korea. The revival of the China-Korea-Russia rail corridor is crucial for the stability of Asia, and is understood by the Chinese leadership as a key element to the entire "win-win" Eurasian development strategy.

There are no viable alternatives to this total victory/total war approach to defeating the British. A German-Russian alliance to revive Eurasia from the European side, as earlier envisioned by French President Gen. Charles de Gaulle, the last French leader to possess a Eurasian vision, is the only option left for Europe and the entire trans-Atlantic region. In the United States, this means dumping Obama, who is nothing but a British pawn, and wiping out Wall Street. In Asia, the China-Korea-Russia rail corridor is critical to a meaningful solution to the escalating British empire war provocations, largely run through the mouth of Barack Obama and directed not against North Korea, but against China. India is a natural partner in this Asia development endeavor, and is already on board, extending the Eurasian development corridors into the Indian Ocean.

Russian President Putin has accounted well for himself in the Russian strategic intervention in Syria, which has drawn the fools in Turkey and Saudi Arabia into a trap of their own making. This trap has caught the British empire crowd off guard, and this is the moment to crush them entirely.

These are the pressing global policies that must be considered and adopted. This is no time to engage in endless debate and procrastinating. These policies must be adopted, now, and effectively implemented. It is the effective implementation that is subject to serious planning among serious world leaders, the majority of whom reside in Eurasia, as the result of generations of British brutalization of the American and continental European populations.

If you catch yourself thinking "Yes, but this is not practical," you are already doomed.

EIR Contents

www.larouchepub.com Volume 43, Number 9, February 26, 2016

Cover This Week

Rason port in North Korea, the crucial hub of cooperation between North Korea, South Korea, Russia, and China,— cooperation now threatened by Obama's war provocations. Lyndon LaRouche holds that the Korea crisis can only be solved by a revival of the China-Korea-Russia rail links that have historically existed, and can and must be revived today.

I. What We Do Now Is Crucial

OBAMA'S WAR ON CHINA

Last Chance To Save the British Empire

by Mike Billington

Feb. 22 (EIRNS)—The desperate effort of the British empire to save itself from total destruction is now crumbling. The measures taken to prop up the bankrupt trans-Atlantic banking system since the 2008 collapse have only created an even bigger speculative bubble, which is now exploding across Europe and soon on Wall Street. Simultaneously, President Vladimir Putin's brilliant strategic flanking intervention into Syria is very close to defeating the Saudi- and Turkish-funded terrorist operations there, leaving Obama and the British exposed as supporters of terrorism as a means of imposing regime change against disobedient governments.

Faced with this defeat, Obama has now dramatically escalated the U.S.-British confrontation with China, putting the world even closer to a thermonuclear war which could exterminate the human race. Using the false pretense that the North Korean nuclear weapons test and successful space launch required a massive show of force,— and the equally false pretense of China's so-called aggression in the South China Sea,— Obama is deploying the world's most modern and destructive weapons along China's maritime border, in South Korea and the Philippines, adding to the extensive deployment of nuclear capable warships and submarines in the Pacific as part of his "Pivot to Asia" policy.

Lyndon LaRouche has emphasized the urgency of restoring the collaboration between South Korea, Russia, and China in rebuilding the rail connection through North Korea, completing the New Silk Road between Pusan and Rotterdam, which will end the Empire's ability to use the North Korea issue to blow up Asia's now central role in the world.

The British empire's control of Asia for nearly two centuries was based on imposing backwardness,— preventing industrialization, pushing drugs under the guise of "free trade," and dominating the sea with its navy to crush any resistance. Now, China is breaking out, with a miraculous economic development process and a "New Silk Road Economic Belt" to connect by land with the rest of Eurasia and Africa, along with a New Maritime Silk Road to establish economic and strategic maritime security.

South Korea, meanwhile, under President Park Geun-Hye, the daughter of the father of the South Korean economic miracle, Park Chung-hee, has adopted a "Eurasian Vision" based on development cooperation with Russia and China.

These development projects are perceived as a threat

Missile Defense Agency

Obama is sending a Terminal High Altitude Area Defense (THAAD) missile system into South Korea, which will be of no use against nearby North Korea, but which will pose a real threat to China and the Russian Far East.

to the empire and, in the view of London and Wall Street, must be destroyed.

Obama's Preparation for War

Obama is in the process of sending a Terminal High Altitude Area Defense (THAAD) missile system into South Korea, claiming it is needed to defend against North Korea. Such high altitude systems are of no use against North Korea, which lies only 30 miles from Seoul, but are a real threat to China and the Russian Far East. The Chinese are quite aware of that,— just as Russia was not fooled by the incredible argument that the deployment of anti-ballistic missile systems on its border was needed to defend against Iran.

An editorial in the official Communist Party of China newspaper *Global Times* on Feb. 17 was explicit: "Once the THAAD system is deployed in South Korea, Chinese society will be bound to support the Peoples Liberation Army to respond via a strong enough military deployment in northeast. If so, South Korea may turn into a highly sensitive area in the game of military deployments between China and the United States."

Obama has also sent to the upcoming U.S.-South Korea annual military exercises four F-22 Raptor fighter jets (the most advanced war plane in the world), an aircraft carrier, B-52 bombers, and a four-fold increase in U.S. troops. South Korean President Park Geun-hye, who until now has fostered close working relations with China and Russia as part of her Eurasian Vision for bringing peace through development in North Korea, has now capitulated to Obama. In addition to the U.S. military deployments, Park has shut down the economic development zone in Kaesong, North Korea, where 124 South Korean companies produced goods with North Korean labor. Members of President Park's

U.S. Air Force photo/Staff Sgt. Amber Grimm

Obama has sent four F-22 Raptor fighter jets—the most advanced war plane in the world—to South Korea, in addition to an aircraft carrier, B-52 bombers, and a four-fold increase of U.S. troops, for the upcoming U.S.-South Korea annual military exercises. Here (center), a U.S. F22 Raptor at Osan Air Base, South Korea in February.

party have even called for South Korea to develop nuclear weapons.

Most important, President Park has closed off the cooperation with Russia for transporting Russian coal through Rason port in northeast North Korea to the South. This project is promoted in the *EIR* report, *The New Silk Road Becomes the World Land-Bridge,* as the necessary seed-crystal for breaking the British geopolitical use of North Korea to destabilize Asia as a whole. The plan was to rebuild the rail corridors through North Korea, connecting South Korea with the Russian and China rail routes and bringing real development to North Korea. Lyndon LaRouche declared on Feb. 21 that this "Peace Through Development" approach to the Korea issue must be restored as the necessary means to prevent the British/Obama drive for war on China and Russia.

As for North Korea, although even China has denounced its continued nuclear weapons development program, I would note that the North Koreans have observed what was done to Iraq and Libya after they gave up their nuclear weapons programs to appease the West,— only to

Location of North Korea's ice-free port at Rason, formerly called Rajin-Sonbong.

be bombed back to the stone age and left in the hands of warring terrorist factions.

As for North Korea's satellite program, experts such as MIT's Theodore Postol have emphasized that the technology needed to place a satellite in orbit is far from equivalent to the technology needed for an ICBM, which must re-enter the atmosphere and be directed to a target. Denying any country the right to a space program is pure technological apartheid.

Recolonization of the Philippines

In the Philippines, which threw out the U.S. military bases in 1991 and wrote into its Constitution that no foreign soldiers or bases would be allowed in the country without Senate approval, Obama's puppet regime of President Noynoy Aquino in Manila has just approved the U.S. military occupation of bases across the country. A Supreme Court packed with Aquino's supporters approved the plan on Jan. 12, without Senate approval, despite massive popular opposition and the clear constitutional prohibition against it. This will provide the United States with bases for air and sea power, prepositioning and storage facilities for the military hardware needed for a war, as well as availability for essentially unrestricted rotating U.S. troop deployments.

The United States has already deployed warplanes and warships from Philippine bases to intentionally transgress Chinese territorial waters, not, as it claims for the testing of freedom of navigation, which China has never challenged, but as provocations to war. Indeed, approximately 90% of the trade passing through the portion of the South China Sea claimed by China is going to or from China, which therefore has the greatest need for freedom of navigation.

The Chinese recognize the danger, and are taking the necessary defensive measures. Several statements

Official White House Photo by Pete Souza

South Korean President Park Geun-hye, who had fostered close working relations with China and Russia as part of her Eurasian Vision for bringing peace through development in North Korea, has capitulated to pressure brought by Obama. She is shown here with Obama at the White House, May 7, 2013.

published in the official Chinese press have warned the Philippines, and now also South Korea, that if they insist on playing as pawns for the U.S. war plan, they may well end up being destroyed.

General Wang Haiyun from the China Society for International Strategy, which is close to the Central Military Commission which runs China's armed forces, wrote in *Global Times* on Feb. 16 that the extreme danger of war on the Korean Peninsula requires that China increase defenses near the Korean border and in the maritime region. He said that the United States was using the crisis in Korea to justify the buildup around China. An editorial in the *Global Times*, referring to the U.S. provocation in the South China Sea, called Obama's bluff: "China holds firm strategic initiatives in the South China Sea, and the United States has no actual effective tools to contain China in the waters. It is at best a rhetorical offensive, so we must reason with it head on."

Is the United States under Obama capable of reason? These U.S. military provocations dramatically confirm the seriousness of Obama's first strike doctrine, "Prompt Global Strike," a policy to pre-emptively take out an opponent's ability to respond to a first strike. Chinese President Xi Jinping, like Vladimir Putin, will not back down to tyranny.

The Death of an Empire

These threats are, in fact, the sign of a dying empire.

It began with the Vietnam War. President John Kennedy had rejected the British effort to draw the United States into a colonial war in Asia, under the guise of combating communism. JFK made clear to his inner circle, drawing on the advice of General Douglas MacArthur, that he would not send ground troops into Vietnam, and that he intended to re-establish ties with China in his second term. He was then assassinated (by the British), and the United States was rapidly drawn into a war which not only laid waste to most of Indochina, but also marked the death of the American System of George Washington, John Quincy Adams, Abraham Lincoln, and Franklin Roosevelt. The United States has never recovered.

The Chinese Miracle

China, on the other hand, under Deng Xiaoping's leadership from 1987 to 1992, unleashed one of the greatest economic development processes of history, transforming a nation battered by the nightmare of the Cultural Revolution, into one of the most productive nations on Earth. Under current President Xi Jinping, China has restored the Confucian tradition of harmony and scientific investigation, while also reaching out to the entire world with a "win-win" policy of infrastructure development through the "One Belt-One Road" New Silk Road program, new international funding institutions, educational exchanges for developing nations, an aggressive space program, and more.

In the eyes of the Lords of the collapsing trans-Atlantic financial system, representing the last gasp of the dying British empire, this new paradigm of global development is seen as a threat, as the enemy which must be destroyed if the power of the City of London and Wall Street is to be maintained. This must be seen in light of the expressed view of the British royal family that the primary problem facing mankind is overpopulation, and that we must use whatever means necessary to bring the population down to its natural "carrying capacity" of one or two billion. Global thermonuclear war would contribute to that satanic aim, especially if directed against the world's most populous nation.

Meanwhile, the man most responsible for placing Barack Obama in the presidency, Wall Street's leading speculator George Soros, proudly announced in January that his and other hedge funds were shorting the Chinese currency, in an effort to break the markets and loot the nation's reserves. The effort has failed.

Obama and his British/Wall Street sponsors are losing to the new paradigm of development represented by China and Russia through the BRICS network. The dinosaurs' last chance for survival is thermonuclear war, which can, and must, be stopped by the constitutional removal of Obama from office, now, and the final demise of the British empire.

THE WORLD NEEDS A PLAN FOR PEACE!

Will Ankara Be the New Sarajevo?

by Helga Zepp-LaRouche, chair of the German political party Civil Rights Movement Solidarity

Feb. 19—If Turkey reacts to the most recent terror attack in Ankara (in which 28 people died) with a ground invasion of northern Syria—formally to counterattack against the Kurds, but much more to "save" the rebel groups which Turkey supports, ranging from al-Nusra to ISIS—there is the immediate danger that it will bring on a military confrontation between the Turkish military units and the Syrian army supported by Russia. At that point we would, in the blink of an eye, have a military confrontation between NATO member Turkey and Russia. Russia would have to find a way to protect its approximately 20,000 troops in Syria, and the conflict could escalate very rapidly to a nuclear confrontation. That would be a third—this time thermonuclear—world war!

Up until now Erdogan has limited himself to shelling Kurdish positions in Syria—a course of action which the UN Security Council has unanimously condemned. But President Obama has made it totally clear that, while the United States would not participate in a ground invasion of Syria, it would decline to prohibit its client states Turkey and Saudi Arabia from doing so. The former head of U.S. military intelligence, the DIA, Lt. Gen. Michael Flynn, has pointed out many times that the White House supports various of the terrorist groups for geopolitical reasons, and it has meanwhile been extensively documented that the "allies" of the United States—among others, Turkey, Saudi Arabia, and Qatar—are the most important supporters of ISIS, al-Nusra, al-Qaeda, and the Muslim Brotherhood.

In view of this reality, Chancellor Merkel is taking a totally wrong approach in relying primarily on a common action plan with Turkey to solve the refugee crisis, to secure its external borders to prevent refugee departures for Greece and beyond, to provide for the refugees on site, and to "combat the causes of the refugee crisis." Erdogan's support for these terrorist groups is one of the main *causes* of the refugee crisis! Merkel's additional proposal for establishing a no-fly zone in Syria, where the refugees would supposedly have a safe place to stay, has been thoroughly rejected by the Pentagon—for the obvious reason that such a zone could only be enforced by military means, and thus would bring with it the acute danger of a military encounter with the Russian air force.

If the EU summit with Turkey, set for early March, is to prove meaningful in any way, the cutting off of support for these terrorist groups by Turkey and Saudi Arabia should be the first point on the agenda.

More important, a whole array of fallacies rampant

Will Turkey provoke a nuclear confrontation between NATO and Russia by invading northern Syria—to protect British-Saudi terrorist proxies? Here, the Ansar al-Shariah brigade pledges allegiance to British-Saudi-owned al-Nusra.

in the EU will have to be corrected.

Europe's Bankruptcy

Since his military intervention on Sept. 30, 2015, Russian President Putin has taken control of the situation—which, as General Harald Kujat has correctly stressed, has for the first time created the potential for a political settlement. Putin is acting from a position of strength, while the state of affairs in Europe, the United States, and their so-called allies Turkey and Saudi Arabia can aptly be described as bankrupt. The latest EU Summit provides the latest proof of that.

The Russian ambassador in Paris, Alexander Orlov, warned during the Valdai Club's Feb.

U.S. Department of Defense/Erin A. Kirk-Cuomo
Lt. Gen. Michael Flynn: The White House is supporting terrorist organizations. Here, Flynn speaks at the Defense Intelligence Agency.

10 Paris conference on the Middle East that the world, especially in the Near East, has never found itself so close to a catastrophe, and that Syria today could become the Serbia of 1914. Jacques Attali has just emphasized in his Feb. 15 blog in the French newspaper *L'Express* that Russian Prime Minister Dmitri Medvedev warned, at the Munich Security Conference, of the possibility of a new world war, and underlined the reality that Russia is still the strongest nuclear power. What Attali obviously left out was his own role in bringing on the crisis in the EU.

In the EU, the so-called Visegrad group of countries—Poland, the Czech Republic, Slovakia and Hungary—have already sealed off their borders; Austria has done the same, and Serbia itself, although it did not want to, was forced to close its borders with Macedonia. Thus, the Schengen Treaty (which mandates open borders in Europe)—and with it the basis for the European Monetary Union itself—has been *de facto*

Courtesy of World Economic Forum/Creative Commons
Turkish President Recep Tayyip Erdogan. How can Merkel have a common action plan to solve the refugee crisis with Erdogan, who supports the terrorist groups that are creating refugees?

eliminated. All of Merkel's contortions to allow special treatment for Great Britain—fewer social benefits for the first four years for non-British EU citizens who move to Great Britain, no controls by Brussels over London's financial center, changes in the EU treaties—will probably not stop the Brexit. By the time of the British referendum on leaving the EU, the EU may not even exist! This EU has neither unity, nor solidarity, and common values are nowhere to be found.

Warnings are proliferating of an immediate financial collapse, which the market mechanisms can no longer control; neither central banks nor governments, it is said, would be able to intervene, and all the instruments which have been relied on since 2008 to prop up the system, have been used up in the meantime, or have proven themselves to be the equivalent of boomerangs.

It should be clear to any head of state or responsible person in the face of this complex and rapidly developing situation, that a "business as usual" attitude, a simple muddling through, can only lead to a huge collapse. Everything—the lives and the future of all of us—will depend upon whether at least some of these responsible people have the moral strength and intellectual integrity to realize that there is no solution within the current geometry, but that we need a new paradigm.

Expand the Silk Road!

The way out is at hand. We have to give up the suicidal confrontation with Russia and China which is being dictated by Washington and London. Without Russia, there can be no solution for Syria, for terror-

New Silk Road: The first Chinese container train arrives in Tehran, Feb. 15, 2016, after a fourteen-day journey from Yiwu in Zhejiang province—a journey of 6,500 miles.

ism or for the refugee crisis, and without collaboration with China there is no way to overcome the economic and financial crisis in the trans-Atlantic sector.

Since 2013, with the program for the New Silk Road, China has put a new concept of mutually advantageous economic cooperation—the so-called "win-win perspective"—on the agenda, an economic model which is not oriented to the monetarist criteria of maximizing the profits of the speculators, but to the development of the real economy. The Silk Road economic model most aptly fills the enormous vacuum left by the neo-liberal system which the IMF and World Bank represent, a vacuum namely on the question of real industrial and economic development, and its prerequisites in infrastructure. It's therefore no wonder that more than 60 countries are participating in projects of the New Silk Road, and are using the new banks established to provide credit for these projects—such as the Asian Infrastructure Investment Bank, the New Development Bank of the BRICS countries, the New Silk Road Development Fund, and several more.

The Indian blog "Indian Punchlines" on Feb. 18 underscored the stark contrast between the conflict in Syria, and the arrival of the first Chinese train along the New Silk Road route from Yiwu in China to Teheran. This train arrived in Iran two days after the meeting of the Syrian Support Group in Munich after a 14 day trip of more than 10,000 kilometers through the steppes of Kazakstan and Turkmenistan, with a cargo of 32 containers. From the standpoint of history, this arrival will prove itself a more important development than the Syria developments.

The only opportunity for solving all the problems of Europe—the war danger, the refugee crisis, the threat of a meltdown of the trans-Atlantic financial system, Europe's identity crisis—lies in collaboration with China, Russia, India, and other counties in the expansion of the New Silk Road to the entire Near and Middle East, and Africa. Xi Jinping's recent trip to Saudi Arabia, Egypt, and Iran, among others, laid the basis for this.

Mrs. Merkel has only one chance for bringing Europe's policy toward the refugee question, which she correctly launched, to a positive conclusion: She must campaign for real economic development of Southwest Asia and Africa, instead of relying on crooked deals with Turkey. That however demands a break with the axioms of the neoliberal economic model and a return to a policy which the late German Chancellor Konrad Adenauer and French President Charles de Gaulle would approve. Germany has the potential and historic mission to overcome the acute danger of war through cooperating with China, Russia, and India to extend the New Silk Road into the region from which the refugees are fleeing war and hunger. Whether Mrs. Merkel decides to take up this mission, or chooses to be a pawn on the Anglo-American imperial chessboard, will be the measure of her chancellorship—and more important, will likely determine the future of mankind.

The solution is simple: The casino economy must be ended by re-establishing the Glass-Steagall law; an international debt conference must write off the toxic paper of the banks; and a new credit system must finance investments in the projects of the New Silk Road. For that we don't need any bloated overblown supranational bureaucracy in Brussels, but an alliance of sovereign nation states, bonded together by a common mission for the development of regions of the world which urgently need our help. Only if Europe returns to its humanist tradition, will we be able to survive.

This article was translated from German.

II. Our Space Imperative

Mankind's Realization of Its Own True Self Lies in the Development of Space

Feb. 18—The following statement was released today by Kesha Rogers, who was twice the democratic nominee for U.S. Congress in the 22nd Texas Congressional District. She leads the fight against Obama's criminal shutdown of NASA and for a dramatic expansion of the space program.

What is required of nations today, in order to come together around that common aim of all mankind—progress? It starts with recognizing what visionary space scientist and pioneer of aerospace technology Krafft Ehricke once called mankind's "extraterrestrial imperative." The purpose of mankind is to chart new paths, create new frontiers, and make new discoveries—achievements not realized by man before. Ehricke knew that reaching the lunar surface would be a milestone in the expression of man's extraterrestrial imperative. The inspiration for Ehricke on the great lunar frontier came at a very young age, when he saw Hermann Oberth's 1929 film, *Frau im Mond,* or *Woman on the Moon.* Ehricke's extraterrestrial imperative saw it as inevitable that man—as a species capable of unlimited development—had to go into space. Ehricke once exclaimed, "Necessity provides the reasons for making space operations a matter of routine. In the next 30 years, the process of converting once alien and hostile space into a useful and enjoyable resource will be accelerated greatly. The discovery of our civilization's many needs for space has hardly begun."

When President John F. Kennedy uttered those inspiring words, "we choose to go to the Moon, and to do the other things, not because they are easy, but because they are hard," he was not speaking of a one-time experience of fulfilling some thrill of competing in a race, like race car drivers, aiming to be the first to the finish line, or wondering who will be the first to plant their

Kesha Rogers, LPAC Policy Committee member Johnson Space Center, Houston, TX

Kesha Rogers speaking to LPACTV on Feb. 1 from the Johnson Space Center in Houston, Texas.

flag on the Moon, so that years later a new President could come along and say "been there, done that."

Kennedy too recognized that mankind has an extraterrestrial imperative, and that it starts with the landing of human beings on the Moon and then continues by further mastering and developing the lunar surface as mankind's gateway to developing the universe. Kennedy understood that this was the interest of all mankind. When the Soviet Union sent mankind's first spacecraft to orbit the Earth, the Soviets charted a path that inspired the world. Great visionaries knew that mankind had a greater destiny in exploring the limits of our Solar System and beyond. Kennedy knew that the United States had to be a leader in this mission; he understood that his call for landing a man on the Moon by the end of the 1960s was the only way forward, despite opposition by budget cutters, environmentalists, and those who wished to push a limits-to-growth depopulation agenda of war and starvation. President Kennedy

Courtesy of Krafft Ehricke

Krafft Ehricke (1917-1984), the visionary pioneer who identified mankind's "extraterrestrial imperative."

also recognized that the danger of escalation to nuclear war—and the implicit threat of annihilation of the entire human race—would only be ended by adopting and implementing mankind's mission to conquer space.

In his January 20, 1961 Inaugural Address, President Kennedy challenged the powerful nations who stood in conflict with each other, saying that they had to begin anew in a quest for peace. He declared, "Let both sides explore what problems unite us instead of belaboring those problems which divide us. Let both sides, for the first time, formulate serious and precise proposals for the inspection and control of arms—and bring the absolute power to destroy other nations under the absolute control of all nations. Let both sides seek to invoke the wonders of science instead of its terrors. Together let us explore the stars, conquer the deserts, eradicate disease, tap the ocean depths, and encourage the arts and commerce. Let both sides unite to heed in all corners of the Earth the command of Isaiah—to 'undo the heavy burdens . . . (and) let the oppressed go free.' "

Where is that conquest for peace and true scientific progress today? One need not look to the collapsing trans-Atlantic system, which is on the verge of a total meltdown, and is doing just what President Kennedy warned against, exploiting the problems which divide us as peoples. That system is now undoing Kennedy's vision for advancing the conquest of space, as we see in Obama's destructive policies with respect to our space program. Those powers insist on placing limitations on

mankind, and refuse to accept who and what we truly are, thereby destroying the advances of truly creative discovery and scientific progress. They are oppressing the people.

President Kennedy's proposal, "together let us explore the stars"—this is just what the nations of Russia and China have now adopted as their purpose and mission. The conquest for peace is now being fulfilled by advances in space and especially the breakthrough developments on the Moon being charted by the Chinese. Those advances, when combined with the Chinese offer of a "win-win" strategy of cooperation among nations, through the development of the New Silk Road and other great projects for the betterment of all nations, go far beyond the reaches of what President Kennedy had envisioned. Krafft Ehricke, if he were here today, would be proud to say that China is seeking to fulfill mankind's extraterrestrial imperative.

But where must our country, the United States, stand today in this great conquest of space? Not with the destructive policies of President Obama, and the anti-science, anti-human, limits-to-growth agenda at the helm, where there is no vision in sight for the United States. My campaign and initiative is leading the fight to place the United States back on the map in the conquest of space—to fully fund our space program through NASA to unleash our full potential. That fight starts with removing the threats to the true progress of our nation—and the progress of the rest of mankind—beginning with the immediate impeachment of Obama and shutdown of the bankrupt Wall Street system.

This is the voice of leadership from a true American statesman, Lyndon LaRouche, that continues to resound and resonate throughout the world today. Just as Krafft Ehricke understood, Mr. LaRouche has come to define that "Mankind discovers more and more aspects of the universe. Man is composing the universe as he discovers. Mankind is a part of the universe; the self-development of mankind produces more and more categories of development. The Solar System will develop new capabilities for man's expression. The universe is a process expressed in the self-development of mankind." This conception of the self-development of mankind in the universe is what has inspired China, and it is why we have a moral imperative to join together in this common aim. Once again, mankind is dedicated to the purpose of discovering mankind's own true self.

The Future We Deserve, And the One We've Gotten Instead

by Carl Osgood

Feb. 18—For the past week or so, I have been immersed in *The Rocket Boys*, an engaging memoir (turned into a Hollywood movie in 1999 called *October Sky*) about life in a West Virginia coal mining town in the late 1950s, and about a group of boys growing up there, who dreamed of greater things than digging coal out of the Earth. The author, Homer Hickam, Jr., became a NASA engineer who made a career out of training astronauts for the Space Shuttle program.

This seems like an unlikely path for a boy who grew up in a West Virginia coal mining town, an area that is, today, one of the poorest areas of the country. Hickam had many obstacles to overcome to make the career that he had, not the least of which was his own father, who wanted his son to follow him into the mine where he was the superintendent.

In some ways, Homer's father reminds me of my own father, who was a hard worker, himself, and just as hard-headed, though, unfortunately, he lost a lot of time later in his life barking up the wrong tree. But I didn't become like Homer Hickam, Jr. I came of age about 20 years later, when the inspiration that drove Hickam had passed, having been taken down by the Vietnam War and the rock-drug-sex counterculture of the late 1960s.

At the age of ten, I was completely taken by the Apollo moon landings—I built models of the Saturn moon rocket and the Apollo spacecraft, and the astronauts that had flown into space were my heroes—but the Apollo program came to an end a few months after my eleventh birthday. With my father and brother, I watched the Skylab fly overhead on a summer night in 1973, and I did a high school science report on the Viking Mars lander, but by the time I was a freshman in

www.humansinspace.org

Homer Hickam as a high school student, standing in front of the entry he prepared with his friends, which was the gold prize-winning exhibit at the 1960 National Science Fair.

high school, the inspiration I had felt at the age of ten had largely dissipated.

I had a chance to see the Space Shuttle *Columbia* in 1981, shortly after its first flight, when it passed through Oklahoma, where I was stationed in the military, aboard its 747 carrier aircraft on its way back to Cape Canaveral, and I still remember the huge crowds of excited people I was caught up in, who wanted to see it, too. The excitement of space travel remained with me, but my dreams of flying into space had long before come down to a much lower altitude.

Hickam, on the other hand, came of age at a time when the future was being force-fed to America. That was the accomplishment of the Soviet Sputnik satellite launched in 1957. Even in Coalwood, West Virgina, the mine company town where Hickam grew up, there were people who recognized the significance of the Sputnik launch and the efforts of the team of Dr. Wernher von Braun at Cape Canaveral, Florida, to build American rockets that would match the Soviet accomplishment.

Part of the Eisenhower Administration's response was a beefing up of high school and college curricula to produce the scientists and engineers that would take the United States into space. This policy was even felt in southern West Virginia, the heart of coal country. Sputnik could be seen orbiting high overhead even from there. Until Sputnik, about the only chance kids growing up in Coalwood had to leave, was to go to college by way of a football scholarship.

With the support of his mother, and of Miss Riley, Homer's eleventh grade chemistry teacher, and eventually almost the entire town of Coalwood, Homer and his friends, constituting themselves as the Big Creek Missile Agency (BCMA), built rockets, not simply by trial and error,— though there was plenty of that,— but by studying the science of rocketry. Their rocket experiments made them locally famous and won them the gold medal at the National Science Fair in 1960. "If you have any hope of understanding what the grand and glorious future holds for all who dare seize it, you must come to see the rocket boys of Coalwood," reported the *McDowell County Banner* in August 1958. Indeed, the Rocket Boys were aiming at the future that should've been, not just for themselves, but for humanity as a whole.

McDowell County, Today

What McDowell County has become, today, is the future that President Obama has given us instead, a future with no space program, no fusion economy, no health care, no education, not even running water for a good section of the population. A 2013 study published by the *Journal of the American Medical Association* reported that the average life expectancy for a male born in McDowell County was 63.9 years, compared to 81.7 years in Fairfax County, Va., one of the richest counties in the United States. Southern West Virginia, today, is at the heart of the heroin epidemic that runs across the entire Appalachian region, as documented by the *New York Times* in a Jan. 19, 2016 article.

A caller to Lyndon LaRouche's Jan. 14 Fireside Chat described the situation in McDowell County vividly. Her grandfather had worked for UMWA leader John L. Lewis (who was "Lucifer himself," to Homer Hickam, Sr.) as a union representative, and she had grown up in the county. "I mean, the schools have been closed," she said, "but not where there are many schools, and some are shut down, but where most of the schools are shut down. The parents actually rely on the schools to feed the children, because they can't even provide them with anything to eat at home. There's one hospital there, which is limited in practice, and this is a place where health care was provided by unions and companies, which are gone and the people have nothing."

"Where the people had formerly been living when the mines were open, in company shacks, people still live in these same places, as they were left, without running water, without proper sanitation, today, in 2016. We actually saw people standing in line with empty bottles, in areas where water run-off from the mountains is being collected, so they can get clean water." People commonly use outhouses because they don't have indoor plumbing and their houses have tarps for roofs. "So in this county where my family was once living, the population was 100,000, and today the population is around 20,000, and more than half of the population is living in abject poverty, and they're actually living in Hell."

McDowell County, the caller pointed out, has among the highest rates of heroin and drug addiction in the entire country, and Obama's response was to promise more drug treatment systems "so he could further manage the people's deaths," she said. The only escape many young people have is to join the military—no more rocket building—only to fight the Bush-Obama wars. "And they only come back to this Hell, where these veterans are committing suicide at alarming rates."

McDowell County has been the victim of an intentional effort to destroy the future. Of all the crimes that Obama has committed, LaRouche has been stressing in recent weeks, the shutting down of the space program was the most egregious. The space program wasn't just a science driver for the economy,— it was a vision of the future of mankind as a whole. Such endeavors inspire creativity in every child. "That's what I'm going to do some day," the inspired child says, just as I did when I was ten. The destruction of the space program denies the child that creative inspiration and denies it a future. By shutting down manned spaceflight, Obama has shut down the future and turned back the clock. This is what is reflected in the destruction of McDowell County, today, where the only alternative to a drug-induced stupor is military service in the perpetual wars of the post 9/11 world. Either way is Hell.

The Future That Could Have Been

That McDowell County's future, and that of the country as a whole, looking from 1960, could have been different, was also indicated by another man who makes a brief, but significant appearance in Hickam's book. That man was Senator John F. Kennedy, then in the midst of a heated presidential nominating campaign against Sen. Hubert Humphrey of Minnesota. Kennedy made a campaign stop in the town of Welch, on the same day that Hickam happened to be there shopping for a new suit to wear to the then-upcoming National Science Fair. By Hickam's account, not many people in the crowd were impressed by the

NASA/MSFC/Fred Deaton

Students' interest in space persists. Here, university students prepare their rocket for launch at NASA's 2012-2013 Student Launch challenge near NASA's Marshall Space Flight Center in Huntsville, Alabama.

promises of the Senator from Massachusetts, but Hickam, thinking only of the future, asked the future President: "What do you think the United States should do in space?" After making a joke about himself, Kennedy turned the question around: "I'll ask you, young man: What do *you* think we ought to do in space?" It turns out, Hickam writes, that he had been giving thought to that very question. He had spent many nights studying the Moon through a friend's telescope and so his answer just popped out: "We should go there and find out what it's made of and mine it just like we mine coal here in West Virginia."

It must have been exactly the sort of answer that Kennedy was looking for. "If I'm elected President," he said, "I think maybe we *will* go to the Moon. I like what this young man says. The important thing is to get the country moving again, to restore vigor and energy to the people and to the government. If going to the Moon will help us do that, then maybe that's what we should do." Kennedy, Hickam writes, "was talking about making the country great again...."

Hickam, himself, never made it into space, because his path was diverted by what he thought was necessary service in Vietnam and other things he doesn't identify. He finally made it to NASA in 1981 as an engineer at the Marshall Space Flight Center in Huntsville, Alabama, the place where Wernher von Braun had brought his Saturn V rocket, and the Moon program, itself, to life. At

Huntsville, Hickam worked with many of von Braun's colleagues, men and women who became his colleagues and friends. He helped train Shuttle astronauts and talked them through their science experiments. Before retiring in 1997, Hickam arranged for a piece of one of the rockets that he and his friends had built in Coalwood, to be flown on the Space Shuttle Columbia. The BCMA, he writes, had finally made it into space.

It's not clear to me whether or not Hickam really understands the implications of what he writes or of what has become of McDowell County, where a promise was made and nearly fulfilled, but then was cruelly taken away. The program that President Kennedy had initiated—perhaps including a little of the inspiration from the teenaged boy in West Virginia who had asked him about the Moon—ran on its own momentum for several more years after Kennedy was killed.

The United States, under various presidents afterwards, maintained the manned space program, but it no longer had the goal-orientation that Kennedy had given it, to drive the country, and humanity, forward in the extraterrestrial imperative that German rocket pioneer Krafft Ehricke wrote so eloquently about. President Obama finished off what was left of the manned space program not only by grounding the Space Shuttle, but also by cancelling the programs that were to replace it. Until those decisions are reversed, the McDowell County of today is the future for all of us.

Every Day Counts In Today's Showdown To Save Civilization

That's why you need EIR's **Daily Alert Service**, a strategic overview compiled with the input of Lyndon LaRouche, and delivered to your email 5 days a week.

For example: On Jan. 7, EIR's Daily Alert featured the British hand behind the pattern of global provocations toward war. Of special note is British Intelligence's role in instigating the Saudi Kingdom's attempt to set off a Sunni-Shia war. This religious war has been the intent of British strategy since the Blair-Bush attack on Iraq in 2003.

We also uniquely update you regularly on the progress toward the release of the suppressed 28 pages of the Congressional Inquiry on 9/11, which would expose the Saudi role.

Every edition highlights the reality of the impending financial crash/bail-in policies that would realize the British goal of mass depopulation.

This is intelligence you need to act on, if we are going to survive as a nation and a species. Can you really afford to be without it?

THURSDAY, JANUARY 7, 2016

Volume 2, Number 97

EIR Daily Alert Service

P.O. Box 17390, Washington, DC 20041-0390

- British Crown Pushing War and Genocide in 2016
- Financial Mudslide Goes On; Monetarist Tyranny Gloats over Bail-Ins
- Moody's Downgrades Portugal's Novo Banco
- Puerto Rico's Default: It's Every Vulture for Himself
- Wide Glass-Steagall Debate Set Off Again by Sanders Speech
- MI6 Mouthpiece Evans-Pritchard Touts Persian Gulf Chaos
- North Korea Tests a Miniaturized Hydrogen Bomb
- Uighur Terrorists Found in Indonesia
- Foreign Investors Are Flocking In to China

EDITORIAL

British Crown Pushing War and Genocide in 2016

III. Fall of the Roman Empire

The Fall of the Roman Empire —And You Are There!

by Tony Papert

Feb 18—Those of you old enough to have enjoyed that television series of Walter Cronkite's, have by now witnessed the sorts of sudden, dramatic, and profound reversals of history which you would never have believed possible just short decades ago. In 1945, this country came out of World War II as the greatest industrial, scientific and military power the world had ever seen. Those of you who are about 70 years of age, as I am, had never seen it any other way than as just that. The earlier, painful and laborious climb out of the last Great Depression, under Franklin Roosevelt, we had to learn about much later. And in our earlier days, that grim picture of the United States of the 1930s, had no real resemblance to the country we thought we knew.

Now we Americans find ourselves in the midst of a live replay of the Fall of the Roman Empire,— and you are indeed there! But it's not just something we are looking at,— we're right in the middle of it. Nor is that yet the end of it. "The times change, and we change with them," as the French saying has it. We are in it, but equally it is also inside us. The rot of the British Empire, from which we Americans once fought our way to freedom,— but, alas, only briefly and episodically.— has returned, and now we are drowning in it. Now we see with the founder of our system, Alexander Hamilton, that the rotten decay of that British Empire is a moral decay,— and we can see just that moral rottenness inside each one of our fellow Americans, and inside ourselves.

As Lyndon LaRouche has pointed out in detail, one side of the British-led corruption and destruction of the Twentieth- and Twenty-first century United States, was the dictatorship over science, and then consequently over thought in general, exercised by Britain's Lord Bertrand Russell. Russell decreed that all of physical science must be reduced to mere mathematics, and fiercely persecuted Albert Einstein as the genius who disagreed and would never accept that dictum Russell has succeeded,— a visit to any so-called "scientific" classroom should convince you of this. As Russell understood it would, this decortication of science has forced a dumbing-down of all thought. Americans have become thoroughly stupefied, just as our earlier great genius Edgar Allan Poe had foreseen these effects. This is why he fought to his last breath against what he decried as mathematical thinking, and against all of the imperial culture exuded from London.

Another side of the British reconquest of the United States was our humiliating domination by the (British-spawned) FBI of the unspeakable J. Edgar Hoover, from the time of the 1944 election, while Roosevelt was still alive, and through to the present. Because of the fear that was bred into Americans, no history of this reign of terror seems to have been written; the most truthful thing I have seen on it, has been LaRouche PAC's interview with former Congressman Cornelius Gallagher. For decades, the FBI administered a caste system throughout the United States, in which only the upper, the "security-cleared" caste, could get decent jobs, or often even any jobs. The lower, non-security cleared caste, was left to pick through the garbage, regardless of their skills.

The red purges of Hollywood and the movie indus-

At left: J. Edgar Hoover with the Kennedy brothers; he was later to murder both. At right, the FBI raid against Lyndon LaRouche of Oct. 6, 1986.

try have been covered in print and on the screen, but no one bothers to add that the same thing was going on throughout the rest of the country as well. When President John F. Kennedy began to return to Roosevelt's tradition in the new era of the 1960s, he was assassinated by,— guess what?— the FBI, on behalf of the British Empire. Then the FBI fired the shot that killed Jack Kennedy's younger brother Bobby, whom Hoover hated, on the eve of his winning the Democratic nomination for President, a victory which meant that he would have been elected President.

Then later, President Reagan, newly elected in 1980, was being guided by Lyndon LaRouche, along with a team of Franklin Roosevelt veterans, towards returning to the Roosevelt tradition in a new form appropriate for a new era. But Bush family circles staged an assassination attempt,— aided by an FBI coverup. Vice President Bush took over much control from the severely wounded President. And the British-FBI apparatus framed and imprisoned LaRouche, and, once he was in prison, seized control of his association.

Now we are in a new and totally different world. China has sprung back from its ten-year-long "Cultural Revolution," a British-inspired genocidal campaign against all its intellectuals. As happens throughout all of history, the world owes much to one man, Deng Xiaoping, for this historic reversal. China has risen up to the point that its unprecedented "New Silk Road" policy and its pioneering space program are inspiring all of sentient humanity, as John Kennedy inspired them in his time. Just as unbelievably, just as unforeseen to anyone beyond Lyndon LaRouche and a few others, Russia has risen up from its British-steered self-destruction of the 1990s, more costly even than World War II to the country that lost the most in World War II. Russia is now a world strategic leader under Vladimir Putin. Who expected this a few short years ago?

The United States and the entire trans-Atlantic region, which is to say the British empire, has dug itself into a deep hole. Those who would pull us out must face the facts as they really are, if they are to prepare themselves to create the new facts which destiny requires. Like Kesha Rogers, they must draw inspiration from China's space program, and the victories won by Russia, China, and the BRICS nations. The prospect of the conquest of space and the Galaxy is required for humanity, and required to re-inspire the American people. In that context, the prompt removal of Barack Obama from the Presidency now, will unleash a surge of optimism which will make it possible to take other immediate, necessary steps.

INTRODUCTION

We Know All About the FBI

Feb. 22—It moved into our house, indeed right into our room, increasingly from 1989 onwards. Lyndon LaRouche and his associates have deep, hard-earned knowledge about all the doings of the FBI, in the same way that the Soviets gained a thorough, hard-earned knowledge of the German military forces in 1941-45.

If you have any doubts about the facts cited in Paul Glumaz's article below, study the interview with former Congressman Cornelius Gallagher. You will find out that Neil Gallagher saw many more unbelievable evils with his own two eyes, than anything in Glumaz's account.

Attempts to document the history of FBI atrocities from the FBI itself and related sources, run up against Hoover's insistence on total secrecy. He insisted, for instance, that "leaked" FBI file information should never be traceable back to the FBI.

Hoover prevented FBI-incriminating information from appearing in FBI files, by insisting that it be kept in other, non-official files, if kept at all. He destroyed files frequently, along with the orders to destroy them. His secrecy mania knew few limits.

Under the code-name "Responsibilities Program,"

wikimedia

Hoover arranged for the heads of FBI field offices to *orally* brief Governors and other state officials on "subversives" to be purged from state educational and other agencies, as documented in Athan Theoharis' 2002 book, *Chasing Spies*.

How the FBI Crushed America's Spirit

by Paul Glumaz

Feb. 22—How has America arrived at its current state of political and moral decay? How is it that American citizens tolerate or even defend a President who routinely murders people in cold blood? How is it that in this, an election year, we are presented with an array of presidential candidates who are either buffoons and blowhards, or who defend the sadistic actions of our currently insane President?

What has happened to our nation? Why do we acquiesce in this degeneration? Why are we so small?

The answer to this begins in 1944. It is a story of corruption, threats, fear, and murder. It is the story of a conspiracy, and at the center of that conspiracy is the Federal Bureau of Investigation (FBI), an evil, treasonous organization, which for more than 70 years has operated to attack and destroy the American Constitutional Republic. Under J. Edgar Hoover, the FBI became a national gestapo, operating on behalf of Wall Street financiers and the British empire. Their paramount post-1945 obsession was to destroy the political apparatus associated with Franklin Delano Roosevelt; then to eradicate even the memory of the Roosevelt Presidency; finally, to ensure that no "FDR phenomenon" would ever again be allowed to present itself on the national stage as a viable political option. Since 1944, it has been forbidden for any Presidential candidate to

public domain

Under J. Edgar Hoover, the FBI became a national gestapo operating on behalf of the British empire to destroy the American Constitutional Republic.

FDR Library

The 1944 coup, which removed Henry Wallace as vice president, led to the succession of FDR by Truman, opening the way for unleashing the Cold War and the survival of the British empire.

emerge as a "major" contender for the nomination who posed a serious threat of reviving the moral philosophy and policies of the Roosevelt Presidency.

The 1944 Coup

By 1944 two things were clear. The first was that the war was soon to be over, and the question before the world was what dynamic would shape the post-war era. Second was the clearly deteriorating state of Franklin Roosevelt's health. Given this situation, the British, Wall Street, and their political networks in the Democratic Party had no intention of allowing FDR's Vice-President, Henry Wallace, to be re-nominated at the 1944 Democratic Presidential nominating convention.

Franklin Roosevelt considered Henry Wallace to be the most competent person in the U.S. government, and had fought the Democratic Party machinery, even to the point of threatening to reject the 1940 Democratic nomination for President, in order to see to it that Wallace was placed on the 1940 ticket as Vice-President. FDR wanted Wallace to be his Vice-President no matter what.

Not only was Wallace an agricultural scientist and a competent administrator and economist, he was most of all, in FDR's utterance, "a thinker." As a scientist, Henry Wallace was already discussing the peaceful uses of nuclear power for the post-war period.

As an administrator, Henry Wallace had run the economic war mobilization of the U.S. government. He was fiercely anti-colonialist.[1] One example of Henry Wallace's outlook was that Wallace would recommend that everyone read Alexander Hamilton's *Report on Manufactures*, and referred to "the line of action so wisely laid down by Alexander Hamilton," in which an ounce of government stimulation or participation would result in a pound of private initiative and enterprise.

The prospect of Henry Wallace succeeding FDR in the American Presidency meant the end of the British empire. The 1944 coup which removed Wallace and installed Harry Truman was a crucial turning point in U.S. history. Wallace's response to Henry Luce's call in *Life* magazine for an "American Century," an American empire directed by the British, was instead to call for a "Century of the Common Man."

It was this coup run against a sick and dying FDR that unleashed the Cold War, the unnecessary atomic bombing of Japan, the revival of European colonialism, and the subsequent massive political inquisition against the American population, its intellectuals, its thinkers, its scientists, its artists, and its genius; an inquisition administered by the FBI.

---

1. For a full discussion of Henry Wallace, see Henry Wallace Would Never Have Dropped the Bomb on Japan, by Robert L. Baker, *EIR*.

National Archives

With the installation of Truman as president, the British took control of the direction of the United States. Shown here, on Truman's yacht (right to left), British Prime Minister Winston Churchill, Truman, Secretary of State Dean Acheson, and British Foreign Secretary Anthony Eden.

Allen Dulles (left) and John Foster Dulles (right), along with Secretary of State Dean Acheson, were the key personnel in the Truman Administration directing the Cold War on behalf of the British empire.

The Inquisition: We Are No Longer Americans, Just Anti-Communists

Once Harry Truman succeeded Roosevelt, the British, through Winston Churchill and the 1,000 employees of the British Embassy in Washington, D.C., took control of the direction of the United States. Dean Acheson and the Dulles brothers, Allen and John Foster, eventually emerged as the key persons in the Truman Administration directing the Cold War, and the coups and assassinations against nationalist leaders in other nations on behalf of the British empire.

Those associated with FDR, like Wallace and William Donovan (of the OSS), were purged and driven from political life.

While Wall Street and its lackeys in the Democratic Party leadership played the key role in seizing control over the U.S. Presidency, it was left to the FBI to initiate and enforce a profound, far-reaching "Cultural Revolution" within the United States. Ironically, given the anti-Communist character of the method they chose, what was done bears a striking resemblance to the later 1966-1976 efforts of Mao Zedong in China. Terror, fear, self-criticism, persecution, and ostracism were tools used both by Mao and J. Edgar Hoover.

Beginning with Roosevelt's death, a wave of anti-Communist hysteria was unleashed, using the FBI as the principal tool. As a result we, the

American people, ceased being Americans and we all became *Anti-Communists*. Being American was no longer defined by positive principles to which we adhered, but rather by an agreed-upon enemy whom we were all against. It got to the point that anything we couldn't understand was suspect of being "Communist." Everyone who started discussing ideas that required serious thought was "suspected of having Communist sympathies." Everything we did in the world was now justified with "stopping Communism." Protecting colonialism was done because "we had to stop Communism." Protecting the Nazis after World War II was done because "we had to stop Communism." The United States went into Vietnam because "we had to stop Communism." This legacy can even be seen still today, that despite all the changes that have occurred in Russia and China, Americans are told "they are still the Communists, they are our enemies, and we need to stop them."

The way this inquisition developed was that the House Un-American Activities Committee (HUAC) would subpoena prominent individuals to testify before the House Committee. They would be asked: "Are you now, or have you ever been a member of the Communist Party?" The Committee members would be illegally armed with the defendant's entire FBI files. The FBI would covertly gather the information, and then would channel it to the HUAC as anonymously provided evidence against the defendant. There were thousands of such high-profile subpoenas and hundreds were sentenced to jail for contempt of Congress for refusing to answer questions.

Publicly, the FBI ran a high-profile media campaign through the House Un-American Activities Committee in the Congress, and later as well, with Senator Joseph McCarthy and California Congressman Richard Nixon. On the covert side, the FBI used the public witch-hunt to run extensive operations to brutally intimidate and destroy key individuals in government, in trade unions, in political parties, in the media, in the military, as well as in corporations.

Take the case of my father Steve Glumaz. This is a typical story. In 1950 he was a leader in the West Coast Longshoremen's Union, the ILWU. He was also in the Communist Party, which by then had been infiltrated and taken over by the FBI. The FBI used its assets in the Communist Party to "snitch-jacket" my father. In other words, accuse him falsely of working with the FBI. He lost all his friends and acquaintances as a result.

Then the FBI approached him with numerous offers of assistance if he would testify falsely that the head of ILWU, Harry Bridges, was a Communist. Since Harry Bridges was from Australia, that testimony would be used to get Bridges deported to Australia under the then-pending McCarran Act, which was about to be passed in Congress. My father refused the offers. With his life and reputation ruined, he ended up leaving the country, as many did in these situations. Had he accepted the FBI offers, he would have been crushed as a human being.

This kind of thing was going on everywhere in all aspects of our society. It began right after Truman took office in 1945. While the anti-Communist aspect of the inquisition reached its peak in 1954, with Joe McCarthy going after the Army, these practices of targeting individuals have continued to the present day. Either through fear or corruption, or both, the intention is to break the person's independent spirit. Those most especially targeted were those with uncompromising intellects.

In William Sullivan's, *The Bureau*, that former high-ranking FBI official states: "During the Eisenhower years the FBI kept Joe McCarthy in business. Senator McCarthy stated publicly that there were Communists working for the State Department. We (the FBI) gave McCarthy all we had, but all we had were fragments, nothing could prove his accusations. For a while, though, the accusations were enough to keep McCarthy in the headlines."[2]

National Security and the Caste System

Against this backdrop of anti-communist hysteria and the inquisitional atmosphere, an even greater and more damaging process was going on. This revolved around the advancement of careers and employment. All persons seeking jobs in the defense sector, as well as many other areas, had to give proof of their unwavering anti-Communism to get a decent job. It was the FBI that decided who could have these jobs and who could not. If people didn't grovel enough, they couldn't get the jobs. This spilled over into the unions, corporations, colleges, and every area of American life. This constituted the beginning of a post-World War II caste system governing who was promoted and who was not.

Perhaps the best documented, and certainly the most notorious example of this "rooting out" of undesirables was what occurred in the entertainment industry, begin-

2. William Sullivan, *The Bureau*, New York: W.W. Norton and Company, 1979, p. 45.

ning with the prosecution of the Hollywood Ten. Hundreds of Hollywood actors, directors, producers, and screen-writers were interrogated either by a Congressional committee or by the FBI directly. To be "cleared" of suspicion, one had to "name names." There was no other way to get one's own name off the list of suspected communists.

It was also made clear that one's career advancement was dependent on having the "right" attitudes, the "right" politics. John Wayne is a good example of this. Simply swearing fealty to anti-Communism was the least of it. It was the repression of ideas, the repression of thought, and the repression of intellect that was expected of those who wished to advance in the world of the media and entertainment, and in other fields as well.

It must be stated, however, that what occurred in Hollywood, as famous as it is, was only a small part of what also occurred on university campuses (where many professors were purged), in the defense industry, in government employment, in the nation's scientific laboratories, in the trade unions, and elsewhere. Conformity and obedience became second nature to those who wanted to get ahead. In fact, it was even common that many low-level job applicants, performing such menial jobs as janitor or sales clerk, had to sign loyalty oaths before they would be considered for employment.

Some of this was later revealed in the Church and Pike Committee Congressional Hearings of 1975-76, which brought it to light that for years the FBI had been working with the news media to feed the public an artificial picture of key people and events. Media companies, such as CBS, NBC, the *Washington Post* and the *New York Times*, regularly churned out stories dictated by the FBI, often with the assistance of Wall Street-sponsored public relations experts.

All political associations were routinely penetrated by the FBI, including and especially both right-wing and left-wing organizations. If anyone aspired to leadership in these organizations, being on good terms with the FBI as an informant was often the key factor in promotion. Some political leaders are recruited to the FBI early in life, and the FBI helps them move up the ladder in exchange for their involvement and assistance. These "leaders" also represent part of the caste system. One case of this is former Vice-President Al Gore who, in Tennessee as a young reporter, cut his teeth working for the FBI in helping to frame up African American leaders.

Over the years this has created a society where those who "went along to get along" rose in society, and those

Al Gore is an example of a political leader recruited early, and helped up the ladder by the FBI. As a young reporter, he helped the FBI frame up African-American leaders.

who didn't were condemned to a lower caste, and a harsher life. This caste process tended to select the least truthful and most unquestioning individuals for promotion, while the most truthful and most questioning individuals tended to be relegated to a lower status. The sociologist William H. Whyte, in his 1956 book, *The Organization Man*, describes some of the changes in the American identity within the leadership of corporations, such that the individual executive had became conformist without initiative or creativity. These changes described by Whyte correlate with the FBI inquisition and the transformation of America into a caste system.

Gossip and Slander

Perhaps the most insidious means of political control is rumor, gossip, and slander. Any individual who is independent and has the potential to become a leader, someone who will not "go along to get along," is targeted with rumor, gossip, and slander. One's friends, family, and co-workers will hear through the "grapevine" that so-and-so is getting carried away about something politically, and that perhaps so-and-so should pay more attention to "getting ahead in life," or "show concern for the family."

Once someone has become active politically, and might be stepping on the toes of those whom the FBI prefers, then the rumors, gossip, and ultimately slanders in the media occur. Some of the most notable examples of this include Albert Einstein, who was

National Archives

Singer and actor Paul Robeson was hounded by the FBI for stepping on the toes of the British empire. Robeson is shown here leading shipyard workers in singing the Star Spangled Banner.

hounded in this way from the time he applied to immigrate to the United States in the 1930's, to the last day of his life. Another prominent example was Paul Robeson, who was similarly hounded. The same occurred with Dr. Martin Luther King. There are countless examples: virtually anyone who is independent of Wall Street and their British masters. The most slandered individual in America today is Lyndon LaRouche. LaRouche is routinely portrayed in the media as racist, an anti-Semite, a right winger, a communist, a crackpot, a cult leader, a narcissist, a CIA agent, and an agent of the Vatican,— depending on the targeted audience. All of this comes from the FBI. In addition to these planted media articles, the FBI deploys networks of rumor and gossip-mills, especially to the periphery or social milieu of the targeted group or person.

Infiltration and *Agents Provocateurs*

It is estimated, according to Trevor Aaronson in his book, *The Terror Factory*, that the FBI, *in this current decade*, deploys a force of 15,000 registered informants. If unofficial and other confidential sources are added in, the number goes up to between 45,000 to 60,000 persons in our society, who collaborate with the FBI. This means that there is one FBI collaborator for every 5,000 to 7,000 people in the United States. What are these 45,000 to 60,000 individuals doing? How many of them are elected officials at the local, state, or federal level? How many of them are working as jour-

nalists? How many of these are in trade unions, in corporations, in political organizations, in criminal associations, in prisons, and other positions? This information is secret. Then there is a special sort of FBI operative called the "agent provocateur." One day in the late 1960s, the FBI "heroically" broke up a plot to bomb the Washington Monument. The organizer of the "attempt" was an FBI *agent provocateur*. This man, who was in his early fifties at the time, had also earlier been, at one time or another, a hit man for the mob, a street pimp on 42nd Street in New York City, the chief of security for Stokely Carmichael of SNCC, and was the instigator of the Louisville riots immediately following the assassination of Dr. Martin Luther King.

I knew this man, and at the time of our acquaintance, he was on his way to prison for instigating the Louisville riots, and then, after prison, he was hoping to retire from being an FBI *agent provocateur*. If one searches the internet one will find case after case of the FBI "heroically" breaking up various plots, all concocted by the FBI. The organizer of the 1993 Trade Center bombing, for instance, was an FBI *agent provocateur*. On March 7, 1971, anti-war activists broke into the FBI offices in Media, Pennsylvania, stealing files which bore the heading "Cointelpro" and leaked them to the press. The revelations contained in these files, combined with the Watergate hearings, began a process intended to end such FBI crimes. The subsequent Church and Pike Committee Congressional hearings of 1975-76 revealed that under the FBI's Cointelpro program, dissident political leaders were subjected to false arrests, burglaries, thefts, imprisonment, defamation of family, friends, and potential associates, unauthorized wiretaps, and assassinations. To facilitate these activities, FBI informants were flooding into targetted organizations—on the alert to record personal flaws, gossip, organizational intrigue, and family, sexual, and financial practices and problems.

Blackmail and Frame-ups

It gets much worse. Blackmail is the "coin of the realm" for the FBI, and this is particularly the case with their targeting of independent elected officials. An FBI agent visits a Congressman, showing a photo, or referencing something either embarrassing or illegal that is known to the FBI, and says: "The Bureau wants the

Congressman to know that we appreciate the good work that the Congressman is doing." It is implied that henceforth, the Congressman will cooperate with the FBI or suffer "unfortunate consequences."

It is estimated by many that most of the elected officials in the country have embarrassing personal matters that may be known to the FBI. Either they have been notified of this by the FBI, or else they fear that the FBI might be aware of them. With the revelations about NSA surveillance that have recently been leaked, the picture is still worse To this day, the power of blackmail is held over the heads of our elected officials. If one wonders why the Congress doesn't really work when it comes to the interests of the nation, that question should be directed to the FBI.

If rumors, gossip, slander, and blackmail prove insufficient to control a situation, the next step is a frame-up. Sting operations and entrapment schemes are commonly used. Often the IRS is enlisted to do an audit to see if there is a tax violation that could be used against the target. It is not possible to list all the persons who have been framed up by the FBI,— the list could number in the thousands. Lyndon LaRouche is one who was framed up and sent to prison. Former New Jersey Congressman Cornelius Gallagher, now 94 years old, and a friend of John F. Kennedy, is another. The transcript of an interview conducted with Congressman Gallagher in this issue of the *EIR*, is one of the best accounts of how this process works.

There were two larger groups of politicians who were framed-up *en masse* because they represented constituencies that were organically "not on board" with the policies of Wall Street and the British empire. One group was that of African American elected officials, and the other was that of labor-connected elected officials. On Jan. 27, 1988, then-Rep. Mervyn Dymally (D-Calif.) put into the Congressional Record a sworn affidavit from former FBI special agent Hirsch Friedman. It was then that the longstanding "Operation Fruehmenschen," which had begun in the 1940's and 1950's targeting African American elected officials, came to light. The reason stated in the affidavit was that "black officials were intellectually and socially incapable of governing major governmental organizations and institutions." The word "Fruehmenschen" in German

LaRouche PAC

In 1988, then Representative Mervyn Dymally (D-Calif.) exposed the FBI's "Fruehmenschen" operation targetting African-American elected officials. He put a sworn affidavit from a former FBI agent into the Congressional Record.

means "early" or "primitive men." Some of the prominent officials targeted were New York Congressman Adam Clayton Powell, Cleveland Mayor Carl Stokes, California Lt. Governor Mervyn Dymally, D.C. Mayor Marion Barry, Massachusetts Senator Edward Brooke, and New York Congresswoman Shirley Chisholm. There were many more.

The real reason for this was that the African American community and its leaders were the sector most resistant to the policies coming from Wall Street and the British empire. Allegiance to the heritage of Franklin Roosevelt, the Presidency of John Kennedy, and the Vision of Martin Luther King made African American leaders a prime target for the FBI.

The other mass frame-up centered on operations called ABSCAM and BRILAB. There were more than 1,200 investigations involving some 3,000 special FBI agents targeting "white collar" crime. Some targeted powerful Congressmen and Senators. Key Senators targeted were New Jersey Senators Harrison Williams and Frank Thompson, and Nevada Senator Howard Cannon,— very powerful Senators. The purpose of these frame-ups of elected officials under the ABSCAM/ BRILAB program, was to remove from the Senate and Congress the key labor-connected officials who were standing in the way of the deregulation of the financial system. If they had remained in office, and without the demonstration of the power of Wall Street through the

FBI in their removal, there would have been no possibility that the subsequent torrent of financial "reforms," culminating in the repeal of FDR's Glass-Steagall legislation, could have passed the Congress. These are the "reforms" that have ultimately led to the financial crisis we are in today.

Ripping Out the Soul of America

Let us return to what occurred after 1945. In a very, very brief period of time, the entirety of Franklin Roosevelt's Administration was purged from the government. Henry Wallace was gone, labeled as a Communist sympathizer. William Donovan was gone. Dozens of Roosevelt Administration officers and policy makers were investigated and questioned as to their loyalty. Key people were actually indicted and imprisoned. The most famous of these were Alger Hiss and Harry Dexter White. It was charged that the Roosevelt Administration was riddled with Soviet spies.

Let's be clear: among the thousands of employees in the Roosevelt Administration there were some Communists. First of all, this was not illegal. Second, the Soviet Union was our ally. Third, there were also right-wing Republicans and many other types of people in the Roosevelt Administration. The glue which held them together was their loyalty to Roosevelt and the vision which FDR had for a return to the principles of the American Constitution. However, what was done instead, in very short order, was to smear the entire legacy of FDR as being soft on communism, or worse. By the 1950s, the twelve-year Roosevelt Presidency was being portrayed as an aberration, something which only came about because of the Depression, and something out of step with traditional American values.

As we have shown, after about 1945 the FBI imposed a reign of terror to turn Americans into cowards. People who spoke up were targeted, shunned, fired, or indicted. When Ethel Rosenberg was executed, the message was clear,— even your family members are not safe. John Kennedy, who tried to revive the vision and outlook of FDR, was murdered. His brother was murdered. Martin Luther King was murdered. The American people became more afraid.

Since 1944, not a single "major" candidate for the U.S. Presidency has called for a return to the policies of Franklin Roosevelt,— this despite the undeniable fact that Roosevelt was both the greatest and most successful President since Abraham Lincoln. Discussing Roosevelt is simply taboo. It is something that one simply does not do if one wishes to be considered for higher office. It is crucial to recognize that in extirpating the legacy of FDR, the FBI has also succeeded in erasing the true nature of the United States, because it was Roosevelt, and before him Abraham Lincoln, who most faithfully represented and defended the Hamiltonian nature of the American Republic.

The FBI and J. Edgar Hoover are not subjects of historical curiosity. We are not discussing here past events of the 1940s or 1950s. What was done then is being done today! What began in 1944 is still with us, and the political/social control is still with us. The ban on fighting for an FDR solution to the financial-economic crisis is still with us. The fear within the population is still with us, now greatly exacerbated by having a cold-blooded killer in the Oval Office. The FBI still continues its treasonous dirty work on behalf of Wall Street and London. All of its methods are still in use.

Hope

The system of Wall Street and the British empire is disintegrating. A new global economic system is emerging around China, Russia, and India that incorporates the same vision that the 1944 coup against FDR and the assassination of Kennedy intended to crush. We are witnessing the equivalent of the collapse of the Roman Empire.

This also means that the power that controls the FBI is going down. The power behind the mental shackles that have been imposed on the American people is collapsing, and will soon not exist. Our problem is no longer an objective problem. Our problem is a subjective one. In each of us is the accumulated habit of an internal policing mechanism which is the FBI. The FBI could cease to exist, and we would still act as mental slaves. It is the spirit of the FBI in us that is preventing us from seizing the opportunities for our nation that the collapse of Wall Street and British empire represent.

It is imperative that those reading this begin to become conscious and reflect on the effect that the FBI has had on the mental processes of one's parents, one's grandparents, as well as on oneself. It is also imperative that one begin to face the ugly reality of what has happened. There is hope, but hope does not exist in avoiding reality. Our hope as a nation now rests on the revival of the vision of FDR and Kennedy. That revival cannot happen if we remain in the mental shackles imposed upon us by the FBI. Recognizing those shackles is the first step.

The Assassination of President Kennedy And the FBI Take-over of America

LaRouche PAC conducted an interview with former Congressman Cornelius "Neil" Gallagher (D-NJ) on Sept. 17, 2014. Excerpts are presented here. Gallagher is the only man alive who was not only a close personal friend of John F. Kennedy, but fought the apparatus associated with his assassination and the assassinations of Robert Kennedy and Martin Luther King as a leading member of Congress. Miraculously, he was able to continue fighting, unlike others who had joined him in the struggle. Even more miraculous, he is still alive today to tell of it. Here, at 92 years of age, former Congressman Gallagher presents his story.

Former Democratic Congressman Neil Gallagher delivering a video message to the Schiller Institute's 30th Anniversary conference, Jan. 15, 2014. He had been a personal friend of President Kennedy.

Part I. The Kennedy Years

Neil Gallagher: I first met Kennedy at the 1956 [Democratic] Convention; I was a delegate from New Jersey. And supposedly, the convention would be open, and everybody had their little campaigns for who was going to be [the candidate for] Vice President. Adlai Stevenson said it was going to be an open convention. And so, there were some people from Massachusetts that I knew from the war days, who were friends of Kennedy, and they introduced us. And we had a little boomlet for Vice President, and I got some of the people in New Jersey and we started to stir things up for Kennedy to be vice president. And it was the best thing that ever happened—he lost. Because otherwise nobody would have probably ever heard of him again! And that's how I first met him.

Then, shortly thereafter, I was elected to Congress, and then we became friends. Then, after he was in Congress, then it appeared that now he was going to get serious about running for President in 1960. So, we'd meet every once in a while, and maybe every couple weeks or so, and maybe have a sandwich over at his office and we'd go over how some of the people in New Jersey might feel about it, the leadership, whether the Governor might be for him, or the political leaders. And so we became quite friendly.

JFK's Intent to Return to FDR

Question: Was Kennedy trying to return to the legacy of FDR?

Gallagher: Yes, there's no question about that. I

Kennedy was returning to the legacy of President Franklin D. Roosevelt, "there's no question about that."

think the policies of [Secretary of State John Foster] Dulles and the standoffishness of President Eisenhower, who had the admiration of the world for his role in the war—but policy was really driven by Dulles, though revisionist history says that the man behind it all was Eisenhower, which is probably true. I think he was probably more of a manager than one who was making policy. I think that Dulles added to the policies of Truman and [his Secretary of State Dean] Acheson and left no room for diminution of the Cold War. I think Kennedy viewed that as one of his great responsibilities, to reduce those tensions.

Of course, everybody was so fraught about a nuclear war. I mean, we're talking about a terrorist plot right now, but nuclear war was the end of the world for many, many people! And I think Kennedy took that very, very seriously, how to reduce the tensions, and not fall into a war.

And of course, he was highly tested, highly tested by Khruschchov. I remember talking to him, over there, when he came back from the meeting with Khruschchov, and I was asking him, "How 'd you find Khruschchov? How'd you get along with him?" He says, "He's a son of a bitch!" And we got talking about it a little bit. And I said, "Well, how did it end?" "Well, he knew that I was a no-good son of a bitch, too, at the end." And then his farewell was, he said, "I asked Khruschchov, 'what's that medal you wore all the time?' He says, 'That's the Lenin Peace Medal.'" Kennedy said, "I hope you're still wearing it the next time we meet."

So, but he was—and of course, Kennedy—Kennedy after the Bay of Pigs, really did not trust the mili-

tary leadership too much. And you still had people like General [Curtis] LeMay and those guys, who "sock 'em, nuke 'em, and get 'em outta there," you know. And for a young President following a great general that was a very difficult course for him to play.

Question: Did you speak with President Kennedy about his vision for the country?

Gallagher: Well, not like a heart-to-heart talk like this. But I was on the Foreign Affairs Committee, so I would be in on the conversations in the White House. I handled, and helped draft the Peace Corps [Act], and you could know where he wanted to go with that. I helped draft that, and then I was the co-manager of the passage of the Peace Corps [Act] on the floor. There's a picture there, with the pen and all, of the signing.

And I also introduced and managed the bill creating the arms control agency [Arms Control and Disarmament Agency]. So, on matters like that, Kennedy was for real, in the question of America's role internationally. And of course, he did give hope to all the young people. And all of the people around the world who had fought in the war, it was sort of our turn to be on the stage, and in that way, he truly was a leader of the world's hope. And the new generation was aware of the problems and were intelligent enough and courageous enough to want to try and solve those problems while America still had its leadership role, and while people still really looked up to the United States. And he was ideal for that period, there was no question about it.

The Day the President Was Shot

Question: Who do you think was behind the Kennedy assassination?

Gallagher: I am convinced, I was convinced from the day after—in fact there's a story right there, that you can work in there: The day that the President was killed, I was in my office, and Bob Michel, who became Republican Minority Leader, his office was next door to mine. And he ran into my office and he says, "The President has been shot." And I didn't have a radio, we didn't have radios in there, and I went over to Bob's office, listening to what was going on. And you know, I'd been shot a couple of times, so I didn't really think this tough guy was going to be dead! I said, I was kidding, I said, "Well, jeez, it looks like we're going to win this election." You know, it was a little like the Reagan thing, later on.

But then, as I was there, my secretary came in and said, "Speaker McCormack would like you come over to his office right away." I was sort of a protégé of the Speaker in those days. And then I went over to the Speaker's office, and there were a lot of people milling around, and I said to him, I said—a lot of reporters were there—I said, "You got to give some kind of a statement here." And of course, he was really—he didn't know what the hell was going on, whether the President was dead or whatever

President John F. Kennedy viewed it as one of his great responsibilities to reduce Cold War tensions in an atmosphere of great fear over a possible nuclear war. Here he delivers his State of the Union address to Congress, Jan. 11, 1962.

the hell it was. So, I sort of draft up, dictate a statement from the Speaker to his secretary. While we're working on it, one of the other secretaries came out and said, "President's dead."

And of course, that changed the whole game.

Now, the Secret Service and everybody starts showing up in the Speaker's office, because he's next in line. We don't know whether there's some kind of big conspiracy going on, and so I stayed there, and we waited now to see what was going on next. And then, the word came through, as to what time the plane would come in. And so, I went out, and the Speaker asked me to drive out to the airport with him. And we went out with Carl Albert, the new Majority Leader, and Mr. Roswell from Georgia, and we went out and waited for the plane to come in with the President's body.

So there's a story there, "where were you that day," you know. In fact, when we got out there, there's some colonel had set up some microphones and told the Speaker that when the plane came in, this was where the new President would come over. And then I looked over to my left, and I see this guy walking up and down, next to a tanker there, a gasoline truck—and it was Bobby Kennedy, all by himself.

So I went over, and then, he's walking up and down, so I walk up and I put my arm around him, and we walked up and down for a while. And, what the hell

could you say. And the only thing I remember him saying, a couple things, he says, "that old man's hand is in this someplace [referring to J. Edgar Hoover], I don't know." And I didn't want to press him, because he was crying. And so then, we just kept walking up and down, and then they got notified the plane was coming in. And then, I went back over to see if Mr. McCormack was all right, and then the plane came in. And somehow or other, I never figured out how they did it, but Booby got on that damned plane and walked off with Jackie Kennedy and the casket.

And then the new President came over, and the new game was on.

Who Killed JFK?

The day after the President was killed, I remember making notes—I don't even know where the hell they are now—I was convinced that if there was a conspiracy, there was only one group that could have brought it off, and that was Hoover. And Hoover hated the Kennedys. He thought the both of them were national security threats, they were too young. And most of all, they didn't like each other, and Hoover was very protective of his goddamned job.

I never could figure out whether or not he really set up Oswald or not. But I became convinced as time went on, that, it's hard to bring back those days, but everybody was communist-happy in those days. I mean, there were Communists under the rug, under your bed, and all over! And this guy, Lee Harvey Oswald had been to Russia. He had been a Marine. He came back. No one ever went into the Russian Embassy—and this came out in the papers when Drew Pearson was a writer in those days, a muckraker—anybody who went into the Russian Embassy, [from] across the street, the FBI was taking pictures of everybody. And everybody who went into the Russian Embassy was investigated.

So here you had a guy who came back from Russia, was known to the FBI, went to the FBI! The FBI investigated him, and was unleashed, and nobody knew what the hell was going on! And yet, there's no way that the FBI could not have been monitoring Lee Harvey Oswald, all the time. Because they monitored everybody! It was an employment thing for FBI agents too—"another guy went into the embassy, put two more agents on him." Everybody was bugged and monitored.

And as it went on, then [there was] the Clay Shaw group down there, that he was obviously involved with.

Here you had, really, a group of goddamned people who had discussed killing the President of the United States! Of which a guy by the name of Oswald was familiar to them on it, and he met with them!

FBI Cover-up

And yet, the FBI found no conspiracy. And they try to make it a joke, that it was just a group of homosexuals down there, playing games about what they'd do with the President if they killed him, because he was such a sex symbol, you know. It was a joke around in those days, that they tried to belittle the Clay Shaw group. And yet, there's no question in my mind that the Clay Shaw group, and this was what [Congressman Hale] Boggs insisted on, that he didn't understand it at that moment, why he wanted to open up [re-open] the Warren Commission.

Because there was no question, that group did discuss it. Oswald was in touch with them, and the President was killed! And they got all of these connections, and yet, nobody wanted to take a look. And when you got a spooky son of a bitch like Shaw involved in the middle of this, from his background, there was no way to know whether they set up, gave him the gun or not, who the hell knew?

But I always thought, there was one thing that I'm sure about, and everybody else was, in that period: Hoover knew every goddamned thing that was going on, everywhere! Our Congress was bugged. I hired a guy from the White House, the guy named Captain Hartnett, he was a Signals officer. The Speaker asked me to find somebody to see whether our offices were being bugged, because we knew they were being bugged.

We took a guy from the Signals office of the White House, he was an Army captain, and we hired him in the Clerk's office, to see what we could do about bugging the Congressional offices. And the conclusion was, there's nothing you can do about it, because the same people that are debugging are the people who were putting the bugs in anyhow, on us. So it was so bad! And the FBI was behind all of this.

And so Hoover had to know what—well, he knew what everybody was doing; that's a general statement, but interesting people. But they had to know what this guy from Russia, running around, Lee Harvey Oswald, they had to know what he was doing. I always thought that Hoover and his special group removed all the opposition: Like in a football game, take out all the defenders and walk into the goal line.

Only Hoover's Group Could Have Killed the President

I think that's exactly what the hell happened, and if there was a conspiracy, only Hoover and his special group could have killed the President. And to this day, I feel that that's what happened. Even more so today, when I think the killing of the President was the perfect sting; that now, just like yesterday, they'll get some damned moron and surround him with informers and FBI agents, tell him how they can get a 1,000 pound bomb ... how would an ignorant moron like that guy they captured yesterday know where to buy a 1,000 pound bomb? And the guy who parked his car in New York: The whole security apparatus today, relies on these stings, where they get these moronic guys who say, "Yeah I wanna blow this up, I wanna blow that up." Before you know it, a whole tantrum: "Oh, you want to blow something up? We'll show you where to blow it up. We'll show you how to buy the truck, where to park the truck ..."

Back in the first bombing of the World Trade Center, you had an Egyptian colonel that they inserted into

New Orleans District Attorney Jim Garrison. Hale Boggs, who had been on the Warren Commission, became convinced that the destruction of Garrison was based on the fact that Garrison was right, there was a conspiracy to assassinate President Kennedy.

those guys who blew that up at that time. The FBI gave them a million bucks! One million dollars, and showed them how to make bombs, and rent the farm here in New Jersey, rent a Ryder trucker. The colonel disappears and they blow up the basement of the World Trade Center in, when was that? In '93 or something; whenever it was, before the main one.

So the whole underground spook apparatus is based on stings and informants, and I am convinced to this day that Oswald became the designated patsy. Whether he wanted to kill the President or not, who the hell knows? Did he kill the President? He probably did. But was the way paved for him? Was the set-up with Jack Ruby another way that put closure to the whole damned thing? They get a wacko groupie, a cop groupie like Jack Ruby .... Jerry O'Leary—he was a reporter for the *Washington Star*—won a Pulitzer Prize for [his coverage of] the killing of Lee Harvey Oswald. When the *Life* stories come out, Jerry O'Leary came up to my house here, and spent three days with us, wanting to know about these *Life* stories, and we became very good friends. And I said, "How the hell did you get into that tunnel, or whatever the hell it was, to be next to Jack Ruby?" He said, "Deke DeLoach put me there." He said, "We were neighbors in Virginia and I knew him very well."

And Jerry got a lot of good stories through the FBI. He was one of those guys that they leaked to. He was good writer, and he was a good guy!

When we see how well these stings are carried out today, people didn't understand stings in those days. But the killing of the President, in my mind, was the perfect goddamned sting, and only Hoover and those guys, the tight guys around him, would know that.

The Jim Garrison Investigation

Question: Did you ever speak with Jim Garrison about the JFK assassination?

Gallagher: I didn't have a deep discussion with Garrison on the issues, but we did talk generally about the assassination, and about this Clay Shaw group, and that these guys were in his area. A conspiracy would have been a conspiracy any place in the country, and any district attorney could have made a conspiracy charge. Yet, they were disparaging Garrison, that he didn't have jurisdiction, and what the hell was he doing, and this was a group of homos, and why are they taking it seriously, and things like this.

The Warren Commission

But by this time, Hale [Boggs] was taking such a beating, like I was taking from the FBI, that he really now began to totally believe that it was all a set-up. If you looked at the Warren Commission, it was the Chief Justice [Earl Warren, Chief Justice of the Supreme Court], and then it was [former World Bank President] John J. McCloy, the chairman of the board, and Allen Dulles [fired by Kennedy as Director of Central Intelligence]. From the House, it was Gerry Ford and Hale, and then John [Sherman] Cooper and McClellan [actually Richard Russell —ed.] from the Senate. That was the committee.

Now, the Chief Justice really never got involved in it. By that time, he was a little shaky, to tell you the truth. I knew him, he was a nice man, but it was inconceivable to him, at that point in his life, to think anything was going on.

McCloy is the guy who did all the work and he wrote the opinion, along with the support of Dulles. And I asked President Johnson one time, "How did you come to put Allen Dulles on there, who was an enemy of Kennedy's?" And he just avoided the whole question. And we were pretty friendly, Johnson and I. But he just avoided the whole question.

But again, if Hoover didn't set this whole thing up, then there was only one other guy who could have done it! And that was Allen Dulles! Because Allen Dulles' job, in Europe during World War II was to run assassination committees, groups, all around Europe, when he was head of the OSS [CIA predecessor organization] over there. So, to this day, I can't understand why they put Dulles on there, because at that time, he was fired, he was an enemy of Kennedy, more than the Cubans did, because he fired him from CIA.

So, there was so much mysterious stuff that went on during that thing! It just couldn't be that there was nothing else to it. There was so much intrigues spinning around, Hoover and the special group.

The Legacy of the JFK Assassination

Question: What was the legacy of the JFK assassination?

Gallagher: Well, the effect of it was, I think it associated with raising questions, deep questions that we had ignored, about the meaning of life, the mortality, and the shortness of life, the quickness of it. Why hope, why plan, when a guy like Kennedy who had it all going for him, could be wiped out in . . . .

Question: When a President could be killed.

Gallagher: Yes, yes. Not only a President, but *that* President! Who was strong, good-looking, had everything going for him. And all the money, and the life— and all the girls, and everything else he might have wanted! But with that particular President, who, when he became President, inspired hope not only in this country and among all the young people, the new generation, the people who were not only in the war generation, but the *younger* people! With the Peace Corps, and that their voices would be heard. And there was a place for them to say things and study, and a reason to live and have a place to participate in their government and in their future! I think that was all wrapped up in Kennedy, and I think it was all blown apart when Kennedy was killed.

How does it compare today? I don't sense that there is that sense of commonality, that existed during that period, among people today.

Part II: The Privacy Committee, J. Edgar Hoover, and the Control of Congress

---

In 1962, Congressman Gallagher, whose passion was foreign affairs, found himself confronted with widespread screenings, polygraphs, and personality tests being conducted on Americans by the FBI and CIA.

My Government Is Doing Terrible, Terrible Things

Gallagher: My office was very close to the public entrance, the street entrance to the Capitol there, and I heard this woman screaming, and she was getting in an argument with the police officer by the door, and she was yelling, "I want to see a congressman! I want to see a congressman!"

This woman had her daughter with her, who had gone down for an interview for a clerk/typist or clerk/receptionist and had had to go through a lie detector test, and they were asking all about her religion, all about her sex life, and all of this stuff. And then when she didn't have an interesting sex life—she was only 17—then the operator asked her, "Well, are you some kind of lesbian? You sleep with girls?" like this. And she broke and ran home to mama.

Mama ran up looking for a congressman. I said, "I'm a congressman. Which congressman do you want?" And she didn't care who it was. And really, I have four daughters, and it just triggered something in me that, "Jesus, can our government be possibly doing this sort of stuff to people?" And as a result, I wrote every agency in our government, asking "Are you giving lie detector tests? For what purpose, where are the funds coming from? What's the training?" And that's really how it all started.

Then there was press on it. I got a hearing held on this, and in the course of about three or four months, I must have got about 28,000 letters . . .

Question: Really!

Gallagher: They were coming in with duffle bags full of mail.

Question: Twenty-eight thousand letters of people who said this is. . . .

Gallagher: Abuses of the government . . .

Question: Wow.

Gallagher: . . . and different things. And really, that really woke me up, you know, about all of these things that were going on, that I never even thought about. I was just a little congressman, thinking it was all on the level, from Bayonne! And all of a sudden, I see my government is doing all of these terrible, terrible things!

'Mr. Hoover Is Protecting Us'

Then, as a result of that, I went over to the Chairman of the Judiciary Committee, and suggested that they look into this. And they wanted nothing to do with it. But again, I spoke to the Chairman of the Government Operations Committee, and said, "Somebody ought to look into this."

And, well, to make a long story short, we held a hearing on it, and as a result, there were thousands of letters came in from the publicity of the hearing, that they were bringing letters in, of government abuses of various people that were going on under our nose, that none of us really were looking at. And one of the letters—I'd read some of the more abusive letters that were coming in—was a woman who went to confession; she was a Catholic. And after she finished her confession, somebody propositioned her. And when she said, "I'm not kind of a girl," he then played back her confession. He had bugged the confessional with a parabolic mike!

Again, I was outraged at this sort of thing, being in the Congress, that we're not watching what is really going on, and what's happening to the civil liberties of our people, and the effect that the new technologies were having on our society. I ran over and I saw Cardinal Spellman, who I had been introduced to by Roy Cohn at a luncheon some time earlier. And I told him, I said, "I have four daughters, they go to confession regularly," it's a sacrament of the Catholic Church. I'm a Catholic. And I said, "What are we doing to protect our people from this sort of thing?"

And of course, he said, "I wouldn't worry about it, my son." I said, "Who *is* worrying about it?" And he said, "Well, probably Mr. Hoover's protecting us."

Well, the only people in those days who really had that kind of equipment were the security agencies, including the FBI. So that was not reassuring. ...

Gallagher's Subcommittee on Privacy and Constitutional Rights

In the Fall of 1963, the Chairman of the House Committee on Government Operations allowed Gallagher to hold hearings on government intrusion into private lives. In 1964 Gallagher made the use of the polygraphs, clandestine surveillance, illegal wiretapping, and monitoring, a national issue. Martin Luther King wrote of Gallagher, "Here is a perennial warrior of penetrating intensity ... who does some-thing about civil rights rather than merely talk about it."

His efforts yielded results within three months: The use of lie detection devices was stopped by all government agencies with the exception of the CIA, the Department of Defense, and the State Department. Gallagher was named chairman of a special three-man House Subcommittee on Privacy and Constitutional Rights.

Gallagher: ... That's really how I got into the privacy issue, because no one else wanted to look at it. The Judiciary Committee did not want to look at it! Because it bordered on some of the law enforcement agencies.

But my concerns were greater than that, and we were not trying to intrude on the jurisdiction of anybody else. I mean, we held hearings then on personality testing; we held hearings on data banks. We got into the business of the Army surveillance system, where you had the military, in collaboration with the FBI, were now setting up a surveillance system and every county in America was reporting, and the Army had all this computer time, because they had the computers and didn't know what to do with them, really, in those days.

So law enforcement then cooked up this scheme about the surveillance of civilians, to see whether,— who was a commie next door. And we stirred the pot up a little bit.

Gallagher's Privacy Committee claimed a victory on June 3, 1966, when his questioning of the Civil Service Commission led to the banning of personality testing in the hiring of employees. That year, his work led to the passage of two important acts of Congress: The Freedom of Information Act and the Credit Reporting Act. He began investigating the plan for a National Data Bank, a central data base of information obtained from illegal wiretaps and other means from more than twenty government agencies.

He first understood the character of what he was taking on when, on March 23, 1966, he found his home broken into and ransacked in FBI fashion.

In mid-September 1966, Hale Boggs told him that Hoover lied to the Warren Commission, that the lone gunman story was a fraud, and that the investigation should be re-opened. Boggs told him, "Hoover and the CIA have bugs planted in the House caucus rooms and most of our offices."

Congress Bugged

Gallagher: But everybody suddenly is scared of the FBI! Is scared of Hoover, is scared of his spooks, is scared of the various people, are now complaining of their offices being bugged. In fact, I was appointed by the Speaker to head a small, quiet group. We hired away from the White House a Captain Harnett from the Signal Corps; we put him on the Clerk's payroll in order to see how we could protect our offices from being bugged. And of course everybody thought it was Hoover on it, and who could do anything about it? And the report came back, the very people that we would hire to debug, were the people who were bugging! It was a small, closed group.

So, you were doing away with even the *protections* of privacy!

Bobby Kennedy took up the mantle of his late brother and was targetted by Hoover in mid-1967. Gallagher received a call from Roy Cohn well in advance of Bobby's decision to run for President.

Battling Hoover, McCarthy, and Roy Cohn

Gallagher: In those days, by now, the only two who were really battling Hoover, are Hale Boggs and myself. And I didn't volunteer to battle Hoover. You know, when I was a little kid, I though the Junior G-man was a nice badge that all the kids in the neighborhood could get. And I thought it was all for real.

But now, when I went down to Congress and Roy Cohn, who was a friend of mine—in fact, I represented Roy when he got indicted—he and the whole board of directors of the *Union News* got indicted in New Jersey for distribution of pornographic literature. There was *Confidential* magazine, and another one named *Nugget*—they were bosomy girls, but they were clothed! But they sold them at Newark Airport in a newsstand, and *Union News* had all of these newsstands in the airports, I think.

And they were indicted, and a friend of mine who was a federal judge, a guy named Coulihan, asked me if I would meet Roy Cohn, at the Al Smith Dinner in New York; it was at the Statler Hotel.

J. Edgar Hoover's agent, Roy Cohn (right), seen here in his role as aide to Sen. Joe McCarthy (left), 1954.

And I said, "What the hell do I want to meet Roy Cohn for?" Because I hated everything McCarthy stood for; in fact, my political career was nearly ruined early, when I was a Freeholder in Hudson County. It was a pretty big job in those days, and I ran and I was elected, and I was one of the big men, all of a sudden, in Bayonne, my city. Now, I belonged to a parish called St. Mary's Catholic Church in Bayonne, and a group came to me and wanted me to go down to the railroad station and meet Senator McCarthy and introduce him at the communion breakfast.

I said, "Why would I want to go and meet Joe McCarthy?"

He's an Irish Catholic. All Irish Catholics are supposed to be for Joe McCarthy, right?

I said, "That guy is one of the most terrible men, running around this country ruining it, ruining people's lives, and why would he even be coming?" And I refused to go down and meet him—and not only that, I boycotted the communion breakfast! Which, you know, every aspiring politician likes to go to those little rallies, we got a lot of people there.

And so, I said, "I absolutely refuse to go." And I hated everything McCarthy stood for, and I guess it was contrary to what you were supposed to be if you were an Irish Catholic from Bayonne. But I had an innate feeling against injustice, and that was one of the worst provocateurs of injustice in America in those days, what he was doing.

And Roy was his spokesman. Roy was the guy that ran,— as a very young guy, as a *very* young guy, he was counsel to the McCarthy Committee [the Senate Permanent Subcommittee on Investigations], and became famous on TV.

And Roy would get all of this garbage that McCarthy would be waving, about 29 Communists, 72 Communists in the State Department; and Roy, who was a very big favorite of Hoover in those days, because as a very young federal U.S. Attorney, he was one of the trial lawyers of the Rosenberg case. The Rosenbergs were the two spies, Communist spies, that were put to death. That's what made Roy a giant in the Republican conspirator politics.

Now, Roy now became counsel to McCarthy's committee, and all the garbage called "evidence" that McCarthy had, Hoover would give to Roy, and Roy was the chief counsel of the committee. That was the basis of it.

So, I hated Roy, I hated McCarthy, and everybody who was part of it. I was only a little county commissioner in those days; I wasn't in Congress. So, I refused to go to that damned thing with McCarthy. Now, a couple years passed, that's all over, and I'm at this dinner, and this Judge Coulihan asks me, would I meet Roy Cohn upstairs; they had a room upstairs. And I'm, "I don't want to meet that son of a bitch." "C'mon! Do me a favor," and all that . . .

So that's how I meet Roy Cohn, and then Coulihan asked me if I would represent the board of directors, including Roy. Now, on the board of directors was the President of the Bank of New York, Cardinal Spellman's nephew, Morton Downey the singer, very close with Joe Kennedy, I mean, these were really big guys, and I represented them. It was a nothing case, and I tried it and it was thrown out. And I never sent Roy a bill on it.

But we became friends in this period. And he was an engaging guy, he was nuts—Roy was nuts, but he had a good sense of humor, he was funny. And we became friends, we had dinner, and we became friends. And all we'd ever do is scream at each other about McCarthy, and "what the hell this Communist crap you guys are still spreading around . . ."

LPACTV

Neil Gallagher during this September 2014 interview. He represented New Jersey's 13th congressional district, 1959-1973.

Cohn Tries to Bribe Gallagher

One day, after I was elected to Congress, he asked me if he could come down to my office and bring somebody with him. This guy was the counsel for the Teamsters. They come in with suitcases, and wanted me to hold a hearing. Now I'm getting pretty well known nationally with the Privacy Committee. And it had nothing to do with law enforcement. I was involved in polygraph, the psychological testing, the MMPI [Minnesota Multiphasic Personality Inventory], whatever the hell you call it, drugging kids [with] Ritalin, the National Data Bank. It really started to grow, about 30, 40 campaigns, the campaign of the Civilian Surveillance System they installed, where the Army was now in law enforcement, involved with the local sheriff and local chief of police, exchanging information, data banks, drugging of kids, all these things. I avoided the law enforcement aspect of it, because that was up to the Judiciary Committee.

Now Cohn comes with Sid Zagri, the guy's name was, Sid Zagri. And they want me to hold a hearing on the law-breaking that the Department of Justice and the IRS were doing, under Bobby Kennedy, as the Attorney General. And man, it was terrible, terrible stuff! They must have had about three or four feet of evidence, of affidavits and all of this. And I'm looking at this stuff, at what the hell our government was doing, and all of a sudden, I'm a little guy, the chairman of a three-man Privacy Committee, with a great budget of $25,000 bucks, which allowed us to have one man on that committee!

And I'm supposed to be holding a hearing on the Justice Department and the Internal Revenue Service, which were now, I could see, were pitted against the FBI. And they asked me to hold this hearing.

And, I said, "Roy, where the hell did you get this stuff? I mean, this is dynamite!" And he said, "I can't say." I said, "Listen, where the hell did you get it? Or we don't talk any more."

Cohn said, "Mr. Hoover gave this to me. And he would request it as a personal favor, if you would hold these hearings." He didn't like what Bobby Kennedy was doing, what the Justice Department was doing, and the IRS ... and I said, "Roy, I can't get into this kind of stuff. I just will not get into it. First of all, I don't have the jurisdiction, I don't have the staff—and I have no inclination to get involved in a goddamned war between Bobby Kennedy and J. Edgar Hoover. That's way out of my goddamned league. I'm just interested in these little technical devices like computers and things that are having an effect on people's lives in this country."

And then Zagri says, "Well, listen, we'll contribute $100,000 to your campaign on it." And he says, "You'll have the full support of the Teamsters on it." And I didn't like the way he said it, you know. I said, "Listen Zagri, who the hell are you talking to?" I said, "If I could hold this hearing, and I wanted to, I would. I am not involved in it! So don't you go talking about any $100,000 bucks or the Teamsters. The Teamsters support me now, in Hudson County, so I don't need you or anybody else!"

He said, "Oh, what're you? You're some kind of a tough guy?"

I said, "No, but I'm not a pushover either. So you

Marion S. Trikosko/U.S. News & World Report Collection, Library of Congress

J. Edgar Hoover, Director of the FBI, 1935-1972. Gallagher on the subject of Hoover: (speaking to Roy Cohn): "And I said, 'F*** you, and f*** Hoover, too!'" That fight resulted from Hoover's 1967 attempt to use Gallagher against Bobby Kennedy's campaign for President, "to blow that son-of-a-bitch out of the water," in Cohn's words.

stay out of this. And Roy, I'm telling you, I am not doing this!"

Cohn Threatens Gallagher

Roy said, "Mr. Hoover will consider it a personal favor. And if you don't," he said, "then, you're not his friend." I said, "I'm everybody's friend, Roy, but I'm nobody's whore." And so I got rid of it.

That was the first *major* test of a fight with Hoover. Now, Roy was not an easy guy to shake off, and they had a couple other things I refused to do.

Now, Bobby's now running for President—I'm accelerating this—Bobby is now running for President, and Roy comes in—I come back to my office one night, and I'm signing my mail, a big stack of mail, and I see this letter from me to the Attorney General Nick Katzenbach, demanding that he come before my committee and bring with him the transcripts of the bugging of Martin Luther King, and the authorizations for the bugging.

And I said to my secretary, "this is a letter for my signature," I said, "Elizabeth, where the—where the hell did this letter come from?"

"Oh," she said, "Mr. Cohn was here, and gave it, and said that you cleared it and would I put it on your stationery for your signature?"

I said, "Get that little son of a bitch on the phone, right now!" And I said, "Roy! Who the Christ do you think you're dealing with? Where'd this letter come ...?" And then, Roy, when he got nervous, he said, "dit-dit-dit..." [chattering] he used to tawk like dat, that's the way he use to tawk, like dat—you know? He said, "I'll come down there tomorrow, I have to talk to you."

I said, "Roy, you've got to goddamned well talk to me!" And so he comes down the next day, I said, "Who the hell ever gave you permission to dictate a letter from me?" He said, "Mr. Hoover and I drafted the letter." He said, "Here, Bobby Kennedy's now running for President, and he's helping all the black people, and here, look, look, right here," and he showed me the authorization for the bugging of King, and it's got Bobby's name on it. And he said, "We're going to blow that son of a bitch out of the water."

I said, "You blow anybody you want out of the water!" and I said, "but you're not going to blow me out of the water," and he said, "Well, from Mr. Hoover, this is the last chance you're going to get!"

I said, "Are you threatening me, you little bastard?" And I went over and I grabbed him, and I was about to throw him out of the window, I was so mad by now. And now, he says, and he's running out the door, and he says, "You'll be sorry! Because if you're not their friend, you're Mr. Hoover's enemy." And I said, "F*** you, and f*** Hoover, too!" And I was really angry about that!

But right after, that's when it started, the whole goddamned thing started.

Hoover's Vendetta Against Gallagher

On August 27, 1967, weeks after Gallagher refused to blackmail Bobby Kennedy, Life *magazine published an article tying Gallagher to the mob. A week later,* Life *published another article implying that a body of a Bayonne gambler was hauled out of Gallagher's basement.*

Gallagher: But from that day on, Hoover never let up on me. Then they floated those stories in *Life* magazine, about a body in my basement, and it was torture, man, for four years; they never let up.

Meanwhile, members of Congress became more and more aware that they were under surveillance, forcing legislators to meet with Gallagher in secret.

How Congress Became Cowards

Gallagher: It wasn't a question that people didn't want to believe this about Hoover. They feared even talking about it, about Hoover. Hoover was a *cancer* to this country, and he was a cancer to the Congress. You talk about behavioral modification: Hoover modified

Tuesday, August 6, 1968   THE MILWAUKEE JOURNAL

Life Magazine Links Jersey Congressman to Mafia

From Press Dispatches Washington, D.C. – Rep. Cornelius Gallagher (D-N. J.) said Monday that a magazine article linking him with Joe Zicarelli, reputed mafia boss of the Bayonne (N. J.) waterfront, was a "monstrous lie."

The article, in Life magazine, tied Gallagher and Zicarelli to an "alliance of interests," alleging attempted "fixer" of the Bayonne police department, dabbling in Caribbean politics, and the promotion of a contraband "cancer

Rep. Cornelius Gallagher

cure." It alleged attempts at reducing government eavesdropping against organized

no comment on the article. The FBI denied reports that it had turned over to Life purported transcripts of eavesdropped telephone conversations between Gallagher and Zicarelli.

An FBI spokesman said that any information it might have was strictly confidential.

In a six page rebuttal, the New Jersey congressman denied that he ever had any dealings with Zicarelli, which related to the ganglord's gambling network. His only connection to Zicarelli, alias

Joe Bayonne, was a routine recommendation written in behalf of Zicarelli's son who wanted to enter a medical school, he said.

Gallagher said that Zicarelli was receiving no special favors. He added that he had written hundreds of such recommendations for constituents and that he would never "condemn a young man's future because of his father's past."

"I reiterate: The charge that I helped take the heat off Zi-

carelli's gambling operations by contacting the Bayonne police is a plain and simple lie," Gallagher said. "It is a lie that slanders both me and the Bayonne police department."

Asks Investigation

Life charged that on June 21, 1960, the ganglord telephoned Gallagher and complained that the Bayonne police were cracking down on his gambling network. That was about a week after authorities began electronic surveillance

of a public telephone often used by Zicarelli.

According to Life, thereafter the congressman assured Zicarelli that would be "no further from the Bayonne police that he had talked to "guy in Jersey City," turn spoke with the pr

Gallagher dismissed article as "malicious" tically biased. The Life asserted that federal grew alarmed by the telephone conversati tween Gallagher and

Gallagher has aske A. Tumulty, Hudson (New Jersey) prosecut grand jury investigati Life article.

"I cannot now disc tail the reasons why decided to smear m and has attempted to my career, for these spelled out in my prosecutor Tumulty. factual evidence of Li cious intentions no possession would be

Johnson Enters Hospital for Checkup

San Antonio, Tex. –AP– President Johnson Tuesday entered a hospital in what was described by his personal doctor as "in keeping with the policy" of an annual physical checkup.

The Texas White House pictured the president's admission to Brooke army medical center there as routine although it did not use that word in the official announce

Press Secretary George Christian said Monday that as far as he knew, the president's health was normal.

The president usually has his annual checkup at the White House which has extensive facilities.

With congress in recess, however, and the Republicans holding their convention, Johnson is on an extended visit to Texas.

confined to Bethesda naval hospital in Maryland while president.

In January, 1965, he was bedridden for what was described as a heavy cold and laryngitis. In November, 1966, he had a nonmalignant polyp removed from his throat and repairs done to the incision from his gall bladder operation.

Christian noted that Burkley usually issues a public re-

Hoover caused wild fabrications smearing Gallagher to appear in Life magazine.

the behavior of the Congress through this guy Deke De-Loach, who was sort of a hit man for Hoover's FBI in the Congress.

He would bring over tapes that they had on various congressmen and said, "We're your friends and we're in your corner," but that meant that they owned them, they owned them. It was tantamount to blackmail. He really was the number three guy in the FBI. And he was the hit man against the Congress. If you stepped out of line, he was the guy that brought you in line over Mr. Hoover. He corrupted more goddamned congressmen than anybody during the Jackson days, okay? But by threat and wiretaps.

An example: I came back one day, and there was Congressman [Peter] Rodino. Rodino was the chairman of the [Nixon] impeachment committee, but he was also chairman of the Judiciary Committee. He was only the number three guy in that thing, and he came over, and he was green. And I said "Peter, what's the matter? Are your eyes bothering you?" He had bad eyes. He says, "No. Deke DeLoach was just in my office." And he says, "Thank God for friends." And De-Loach gives him tapes, and says, "You know, Congressman, we've got these bad guys in Newark saying things about you, how you're selling immigration legislative private bills for $200—but we don't believe anything like that now. Here, you take these tapes." And he gave them to him. Now, you know from that minute on, they own Rodino, darn it.

Now, I'm curious, because I'm in a war with these

sons of bitches. At least seven or eight people on that Judiciary Committee, the only ones who supervised the,— they had done the same thing with tapes and threats, and whatever the hell it was. So that was DeLoach.

Corruptors of Congress Tied to JFK Assassination

Incidentally, DeLoach is the guy who put Jerry O'Leary, who won the Pulitzer Prize for [the story of] the killing of Lee Harvey Oswald, put him in the tunnel next to Lee Harvey Oswald. And put him next to Jack Ruby, when Lee Harvey Oswald was killed. So this was one of the biggest goddamned operators in the whole spook community.

It was Hoover's people that got Ruby those credentials. It was Hoover's people that put Ruby there.

And that was the way that worked in those days. It wasn't only him. As a result of that, I began to do another little bit of spade work, of how many people were approached in the Congress. Now, most of the members in the Congress had nothing to do with this sort of thing, and they didn't know it was going on. If you were on the Agricultural Committee and Steering Committee, or whatever it was, you had no reason to know about this. But if you were on the Appropriations Committee, who funded the FBI, or the Justice Department, you were in it! If you were on the Judiciary Committee, or in the top leadership, you came under their umbrella and under their threats.

And there was another very decent man in the Congress, who could have moved up on the committee, but he was the Oversight Committee for the FBI, and he was told, stay where you are. So, if somebody would write in about an abuse of the FBI by Hoover or something, it was referred to his subcommittee. And of course, he being an ex-FBI man himself, that was the end of it! And that's the way it worked. There was no forum.

I had never really said much before, but, when we were trying to figure out how to debug our offices, and

FBI Special Agent Cartha "Deke" DeLoach. Gallagher: "This guy Deke DeLoach ... He really was the number 3 guy in the FBI. And he was the hit man against the Congress. He corrupted more goddamned Congressmen than anybody during the [President Andrew] Jackson days, okay? But by threat and wiretaps. DeLoach oversaw the investigation into the assassination of Martin Luther King.

what to do about the six or eight cases that we *knew* Hoover was bugging those offices, we had [something] like cells. You wouldn't have meetings with a lot. You're talking about maybe three or four people that you trusted, and say, "What in hell can we do about this?" Because there weren't too many people you could trust there, who had the connections. They were under the gun, or being extorted by Hoover and his guys, to control the Congress! And I'm not exaggerating when I say, "control the Congress"! The top three or four people on that Judiciary Committee, they were owned by Hoover, darn it.

Congress Terrorized

Poor [New York Congressman] Manny Celler was scared to death, as in the case of my personal experience with him in our Privacy Committee. So, the way that they controlled,— the only guy on that committee that Hoover would ever talk to, in both houses, was John Rooney of New York. He was chairman of the subcommittee on Justice and State Department expenditures. And Hoover would just go into his office, and Rooney would give him 110 percent of everything that he asked for, and thank him very much for the honor of Mr. Hoover appearing before his committee. I mean, they owned John Rooney. But nobody else in Congress, he ever had to report to. Rooney had three men on the committee. One of them died, and a new member, who was a good friend of mine, named John Slack from West Virginia, was appointed, because he had been Attorney General in West Virginia. It was a three-man subcommittee under Rooney.

One day Mr. Hoover came in [to the subcommittee], Rooney was falling all over him, as usual, and then he says to Slack, "Do you have any questions?" And Slack asked Hoover a couple questions, innocuous questions! The next day, Rooney got a hold of me and said, "Hey you and that Slack are friendly, aren't ya?" I said, "Yeah, we're friendly."

"You better warn him: Mr. Hoover wants him to know when he comes before that committee, to keep his goddamned mouth shut!" And he said, "I don't like the impertinence of him asking me questions in there." And he said, "If he doesn't settle down, he's going to have a lot more trouble in his goddamned district than he can handle!"

That was the way they operated! That was the way they operated: I mean, this is the Congress of the United States! That this terrible man is modifying our behavior and our thinking, and our ability to protect the people that elected us!

Attacks on Gallagher Escalate

Gallagher's victories continued: In July 1968, he exposed the danger of a National Data Bank plan, comparing it with Hitler's census. Gallagher asked President Johnson to stop its implementation and the next day it was killed. Days later, he spotted a man sitting outside his house, pointing a parabolic microphone in his direction.

Weeks after the June 6, 1968 assassination of Bobby Kennedy, Life *magazine published another article, this time claiming that Gallagher personally removed a dead body from his basement. Roy Cohn then delivered another message to Gallagher.*

Gallagher: Now I win the [Democratic] primary, and now, I've got four months to go before the election, which, if you win the nomination, normally, you would win in Hudson County, it's Democratic.

So now, I get a call from my lawyer in the middle of this war, and he says "Neil, you've got to meet me at Newark Airport, right away, right away!"

"I'm in Washington." He says, "You got to do this, please." So I say, "Okay, I'll grab the shuttle." And I go to grab the shuttle, and I meet Larry Weichsel [as heard —ed.], a good friend of mine, and with him is Roy Cohn, and they were friends—I knew they were friends, in fact that's probably how I met Larry—and a good friend of mine, named Neil Walsh. And they said they had just had a meeting in New York with Deke DeLoach, Cartha DeLoach.

Larry says, "Neil, I hate to tell you this, but you really have got to resign." I said, "Why do I have to resign? I just won the goddamned primary after all these *Life* stories and all."

He says, "Well, if you don't resign, Mr. Hoover wants you out of Congress in seven days. And if you don't resign in seven days, there's going to be another story in *Life* magazine, about your wife." And this supposed body in my basement, darn it, that he died sleeping with my wife. And he was living in my house five days a week, and died of a heart attack having intercourse with my wife. And my whole family's a bunch of goddamned pigs, I got four daughters, my mother-in-law lives with me, and my wife, and now, they're going to put another *Life* story in, about this.

So, and then Roy is with them, confirming it. Neil Walsh, who is a good friend of mine, he's confirming that he was at the meeting, and that DeLoach said this.

Well, by now—I don't care what the hell they're saying about me, it's politics—but now picking on my wife, who was a lovely, lovely woman, and my four daughters, who are all "a bunch of goddamn pigs." I said, OK.

Gallagher Sticks it to Cohn and Hoover

So then the next day, I'm up here in Jersey and I met Roy in New York, and I said, "Roy, I want you to check this letter." And he said "Neil, you're doin' the right thing, I know Ricky"—and he did, he knew my wife, we were social friends by that time. And he said "you're doing the right thing resigning." I said, "Roy, you just check this," I said, "You're a pretty smart guy. And just check it for grammar and punctuation, see if there's anything wrong with it." And he reads it, and he throws it up in the air and he screams, "God! You can't say this, you can't say this kinda stuff!" And I said, "It's a letter—now, here's the speech I'm making." I said, "because I've got three more months left in Congress, even if I lose the November election." And every day, every congressman can make a speech at 12 o'clock noontime, and insert speeches, revise and extend their remarks. And I said, "I am making that goddamned speech every single day."

And the speech was, "I am no judge of any person's sexual mores, or sexual proclivities," and I said "if two people of the same sex figure that's the way they want to live their lives, that is not up to me to judge them. But," I said, "on the other hand, the Director J. Edgar Hoover, and the Deputy Director, Clyde Tolson," I said, "have spent 31 years together, having dinner and breakfast every single day of their lives. And now they go around the country, always go to some racetrack together, and they have armored cars picking them up, and all of this is done at government expense.

"Now, their sex lives is no great interest to me—

Gallagher threatened to turn the tables on Hoover and his sex partner, Associate FBI Director Clyde Tolson.

though it is an interesting sex life—but I'm not judging them. But I do feel, as a member of the Government Operations Committee, that we have to look into this whole thing and hold a hearing, as to why these expenditures by the FBI should be paying for these two men to be living in the same hotel rooms at night, going to the race tracks together (which they did), and wearing the same hats. I don't know if the Government Operations Committee is paying for the hats or not." And I really stuck it to 'em.

And Roy's going crazy! He said, "Jesus Christ! You can't say this kinda stuff about Mr. Hoover!" I said, "Why not?" He said, "Well, where'd ya get all of this?" I said, "you know, Roy, this has been around a long time!" And I said, "So I'm just putting together a lot of the stories that I've heard about these two guys for a long time." And he said, "yooooouuuu ca-can't say that!"

"Well," I said, "I'll make it up, like they made up with the *Life* stories." I said, "I have the privilege, and that I can say any goddamned thing I want. And every day between now and next January, when my term ends, I will be making this goddamned speech, with additional facts—or fictions—it doesn't make a goddamned difference to me! But I will drive that old bastard into a heart attack, long before I finish Congress. And you can go and tell 'em: If I hear one goddamned

word, about my wife or anything! So I'm not resigning!"

And Roy said, "You think I'm crazy?! To tell Mr. Hoover this?" I said, "Oh yeah, I forgot to tell you, Roy." I said, "I have an addendum to that letter: "I asked Mr. Roy Cohn to check this for accuracy—the good friend of Mr. Hoover to check my speech as to accuracy, if there's anything in there that's untrue. And I'd appreciate very much if Mr. Cohn would point these out. Mr. Cohn failed to deny it, and therefore I add this to the speech." He said, "You son of a bitch!"—he's going all crazy.

And I said, "What's gonna happen after you're in there that you didn't help your buddy Hoover, now? Right? When I make these speeches?"

So, that's how the hell I got them to back off. Anyhow, the next day, I'm up in the country—we had a house over,— about 20 miles from here. They fly a guy up, an FBI guy that I knew. "Mr. Hoover wants to know why you're mad at him." I said, "Jim, you're kidding! That son of a bitch, after all those stories!" He said, "Well, what can we do?" I said, "Jim, I'm not telling you what you can do and what you can't do. But I just want to tell you one thing, if I hear one goddamned word out of that old bastard about my wife or about my kids," I said, "he's finished!" And I said, "I am going to make this speech starting Monday, when the House comes into session."

"Oh, wait, wait, wait!" and he said, "what if I get him to back off?" I said, "I don't give a shit whether he backs off or he doesn't back off." I said, "This is what I'm doing."

Anyway, to make the long story short, they got the Speaker and everything, and Hoover backs off: They put out denials about the body in the basement, and all that kinda stuff. But then Nixon got in, and the whole thing started all over again.

The Trail of the Assassins

In 1968 Gallagher was uncovering the most damning secrets of all. His investigations led into govern-

Harvard University Archives

Dr. Henry Alexander Murray, Harvard psychologist. Gallagher: "Harvard was getting more money from the DIA and CIA ... doing these experiments on people ... [T]here was a Dr. Murray, who knew how to get all of these grants ... to make more perfect assassins and spies. ...[T]hey would take these young geniuses and give them $15 a week, to become subjects ... One of them was Kaczynski ..."

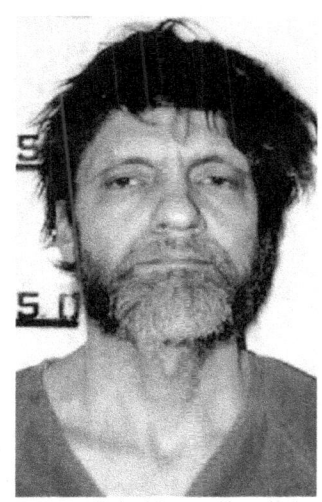

Federal Bureau of Investigation

Booking photo of mathematics professor Theodore Kaczynski, the Unabomber, arrested in 1996 after an 18-year career as a terrorist who killed and maimed in his back-to-nature campaign against industrialization.

ment programs for behavioral modification, hypnosis, and other forms of manipulation of the men who assassinated the Kennedy brothers and Martin Luther King.

Gallagher: So, there was so much of this that was going on! And nobody wanted to do anything about it. Or it wasn't that they didn't want to do anything about it, it was—there was no official forum to consider these things, like the National Data Bank. I think I held some 22, 23 various hearings on this, including what was going on up at Harvard, where Harvard was getting more money from the Defense Intelligence Agency and the CIA than they were getting [from] tuition during those days—doing these experiments on people—the [Timothy] Leary experiments, the [B.F.] Skinner experiments; Skinner, who raised his child in his box, got a $3 million grant from the government, to do studies on behavioral modification.

Question: Really?

Gallagher: In fact, one of the fallouts of some of these Harvard studies was, there was a Dr. [Henry Alexander] Murray, who knew how to get all of these grants on the drugging and the modification of the mind, in order to make more perfect assassins and spies. One of

the abortions of that program, was where they would take these young geniuses and give them $15 a week to become subjects of his experiments. One of them was [Theodore] Kaczynski the Unabomber! And I think there were five or six of these super-intelligent mathematicians—I think one or two of them committed suicide; Kaczynski became the mad Unabomber. And I think the only one that survived is a dishwasher out there in, last I looked at it, in California.

But all of these things were going on at Harvard, and the Leary drug experiments were going on As part of that, somebody was thrown out of the window in New York [Dr. Frank Olson]. He was one of the leaders of one of these programs, who fell out of the window.

I mean, there were so many things going on below the surface of what we thought was the Great American Way, and here was Congress, really, didn't want to see it.

All of these people, who killed the three of them, all of them denied it, and it was consistent with the studies that were going on, and the experiments that were going on up there in Harvard, in making assassins and making spies and making different soldiers. I think it was Henry Murray, the Murray experiments were to produce *exactly* those kind of people! Which is where Kaczynski the Unabomber,— he was one of the abortions of it!

So, nobody wants to make that connection, that we really *built* people to do things like that. But the connection was there. We spent millions of dollars in grants up in the Harvard studies, to create people that would do those kinds of things, and not know it! Sure! But nobody paid any attention to it. I've never seen anybody else make the connection on it. Hale Boggs was convinced it was a conspiracy, but Hale didn't make the connection with the Harvard studies, where we were *producing*, we were *experimenting* to make those kind of robotic soldiers, of the mind or something. I made that connection. Nobody paid any attention to it!

Hale Boggs' Mission to Dump Hoover

In April 1971, Congressman Hale Boggs met again with Gallagher, telling him the repairman found his phone bugged. The next morning Hale Boggs called for Hoover's resignation on the floor of the Congress.

"The time has come for the Attorney General to ask for [Hoover's] resignation. When the FBI taps the telephones of members of this body and the Senate, it stations agents on campuses, when the FBI adopts the tac-

tics of the Soviet Union and Hitler's Gestapo, it is time, it is way past time, Mr. Speaker, that the present director no longer be the director. I ask again now that you have enough courage to demand the resignation of this man." —Hale Boggs

Boggs' mission to bring down Hoover was in parallel with his attempt to re-open the investigations into the assassinations of the Kennedys and Martin Luther King.

Gallagher: Well, by this time, Boggs now sees me as an ally and we were friends. There was a possibility that if Hale moved, I was going to be House Whip in a leadership role down there. [Boggs was House Majority Whip, 1962-1971; in 1971 he moved up to House Majority Leader. —ed.]

Now, Hale Boggs started to make speeches about this [the assassination investigations], too. And Hale Boggs, by this time,— he had been one of the seven people on the Warren Commission, that held a hearing on the Kennedy assassination.

Now, he and Jim Garrison were classmates in law school. They were from Louisiana. Hale was from there, and Garrison. Hale became convinced that there was a little razzmatazz went on, and that the very issues that might bring the truth out on the assassination were obscured. He then talked about re-opening the Warren Commission. Hale became quite adamant about it, and he was convinced that the destruction of Jim Garrison was based on the fact that Garrison was *right*, there *was* a conspiracy, and that conspiracy to assassinate the President took place within his jurisdiction.

And frankly, if you look at conspiracy indictments today, that would have been a home run, and an easy one.

In a 1992 interview, Edward Haggerty, the Judge in the Clay Shaw trial, said of Shaw: "I believe he was lying to the jury. ... I think Shaw put a good con job on the jury."

The JFK Cover-up

Gallagher: But no one wanted to get involved, and finally Garrison brought the charges against Clay Shaw, that Clay Shaw group. And to this day, it remains a mystery: Here you had this group down there, everybody admits they discussed killing the President. Everybody admits that Lee Harvey Oswald and [David] Ferrie, the

In April 1971 Hale Boggs—then House Majority Leader—called for Hoover's resignation from the floor of Congress. He sought to re-open the investigations of the assassinations of JFK, RFK, and MLK. In October 1972, the plane in which Boggs was traveling disappeared in Alaska.

pilot with the red wig, flew to Cuba. Nobody doubts that Oswald was under the surveillance of the FBI from the day he came back [from Russia]. And yet, how could he have done all of this without maybe the path being cleared for him.

And I think Hale now began to feel this way. Hale was battered around very badly by Hoover and De-Loach, like I was. And Hale nearly had a breakdown as a result of it.

On April 26, 1971, Gallagher's Subcommittee on Privacy was shut down. He directed his efforts toward drafting a bill that would create a permanent committee. On the day that Gallagher brought his Privacy Bill to the House on February 8, 1972, Hoover intervened.

Gallagher: So, this was a bipartisan effort: Before I even started this, I went to Gerry Ford, who was then Minority Leader, who was one of the most decent men ever in the goddamned Congress, or ever in the White House, incidentally. And because, now, since I was getting a lot of press on this stuff, so every day, when there would be a roll call, different members of the Congress would be coming up and saying, "Neil, Jesus, this happened to my city, or this happened to my town." Or, "listen to this story" or ... so I was being inundated with this stuff!

I went over to Gerry, and I said, "Gerry, talk to your guys! I mean, we really should do something about this! The Judiciary Committee won't touch it, but," I said, "we're living in a new world! An evolutionary world of technology, that's affecting the democratic process! People's lives!" And Gerry agreed with it. We worked on that, I don't know, for several months, and we come up with a bill—bipartisan; he said he'd support it. And I worked out with Manny Celler, the chairman of the Judiciary Committee, that they had certain reservations on turf grounds, jurisdictional grounds, and we worked the whole thing out, and that's how we obtained a rule, to bring the bill to the floor—in itself it was a great accomplishment, even to get the rule on it. And that included old Judge goddamned Smith down there in Virginia, and we really had good bipartisan support for all of this.

White House/Cecil W. Stoughton

The Warren Commission was controlled by Allen Dulles (third from right) and John J. McCloy (extreme left). On the far right, Hale Boggs. Gallagher: "If Hoover didn't set this whole thing up, then there was only one other guy who could have done it! And that was Allen Dulles! Because Allen Dulles' job in Europe during World War II was to run assassination committees."

More Blackmail

So, the day the bill came up, we're ready to start the debate, and it's going to go through because we've got all the votes we need. And Celler came over to me and he said, "Neil, I'm sorry." I said, "What do you mean, you're sorry?" He said, "I have to break my word, and I don't like to break my word." I said, "What do you mean?" He said, "I have to oppose it, on jurisdictional grounds." He said, "The committee's going to oppose it." I said, "How the hell could you do this, at the last minute? We're on the floor here!" He said, "I got a personal call from Mr. Hoover. I'm telling you why! Because I like you, and like this idea."

He said, "I got a personal call this morning from Mr. Hoover who said that if I do not oppose that bill on jurisdictional grounds, that they're going to indict my brother." Because they had a law practice in New York; on one door was the brother, and the other was Manny. So he said, "I *have* to oppose it." He said, "I hope you understand." I said, "Well, I understand what you're

saying, but," I said, "it's incomprehensible to me, that something like this could happen in the goddamned Congress."

And I think they had 36 members in that committee: Only four of them voted for my bill, and the rest of them ... opposed. So, there was no way we could pass on the bill.

And I'll never forget, Gerry Ford coming over and saying, "Neil," he said, "I gave you my word I was going to support the bill." He said, "It's going down." He said, "You want me to vote for it, I'll keep my word and I'll vote for it, but," he said, "if you want to relieve me of my word, it will help me in my district if I oppose the bill rather than to vote for it." That's a law enforcement kind of thing.

I said, "No, it's going down, what the hell's the difference?" And he did, which I always remember that. It was a wonderful gesture.

And that was the *last* attempt, to set up *any* kind of a permanent committee, that would consider the impact of the new technology on the civil liberties of the American people, and their civil rights. We were talking about civil rights, but at the same time, we were taking away the rights of *everybody* during those days, in a nice, quiet manner, by nobody accepting responsibility for the dehumanization that was going on, on the personal lives of everybody in the country.

Gallagher Indicted, Fights Back

On April 10, 1972, a federal grand jury indicted Gallagher on charges of conspiracy, perjury, and federal income tax evasion.

Gallagher went to the floor of the Congress and, for the first time, put forward the details of the filth thrown at him under orders from Hoover, the origin of the Life *magazine articles, the broad intimidation of Congress, and the incredible revelations that had been presented to his subcommittee regarding U.S. Army, FBI, and CIA abuses of constitutional rights against Americans. He called for Hoover's resignation, or firing.*

Months later, on October 18, 1972, it was reported that the plane carrying Hale Boggs had disappeared in Alaska.

No one in Congress questions his five years of trying to expose the JFK assassination.

He had become the House Majority Leader of the U.S. Congress.

Boggs Disappeared

Gallagher: I always thought they blew the plane up. I always thought that. Because Hale was starting to make a lot of noise, like I did, although he was a more serious guy, because he had been on the Warren Commission. He came back, and wanted to re-open the Warren Commission, and then this plane mysteriously blew up. And those guys were not against things like that.

Did somebody blow his goddamned plane up? Why not! They couldn't shut him up! They shut me up! They dismembered my seat in the Congress: They indicted me—there was never any corruption, or payoffs, or bribes, or anything. The judge said that. They indicted me, and the next day, they dismembered my Congres-

Congress was "a willing victim" of FBI corruption, "because everybody was scared, because the New York Times v. Sullivan *case said you can lie about politicians. They eliminated all slander and libel laws. That became the threat to democracy, where elected officials were now frail vessels. ..."*

sional District; I had five cities. They gerrymandered me out of Congress, and gave each one of my cities to an incumbent. How the hell could you beat an incumbent on it, when you only have one little city on it?

They never let up on Hale Boggs either, never! And to this day, nobody knew what the hell blew up Hale Boggs' plane either. But Hale was a bigger threat to them than I was, because he was Majority Leader, and Hale's plane mysteriously blew up in Alaska. So there were very, very strange things going on this country, below the level of appearances.

Congress a Willing Victim

And the congress was a *victim* of it! A willing victim, because everybody was scared, because the *New York Times v. Sullivan* case said you can lie about politicians. They eliminated all slander and libel laws. This put another great tool in the hands of law enforcement. Because you're an agent at one desk, you can write an anonymous letter to me at the next desk. That's enough to start an investigation on somebody. And that's the way it worked. And then you could leak that there's an investigation going on to *Life* magazine or *Look* magazine, or somebody like that. That became the *threat* to democracy, where elected officials were now frail vessels, where with the slightest opposition to an agency, that agency could leak a story out to the new world of investigative reporters.

Hoover died on May 2, 1972, just two weeks after Gallagher had gone before the House, calling for his impeachment. Despite his death, Boggs inspired Congressmen Allard Lowenstein and Frank Church to reopen the investigation of the assassinations, leading to the 1975 Church Committee on Assassinations and the 1976-1978 House Select Committee on Assassinations.

Days before he was scheduled to testify before the Church Committee on Assassinations in 1975, mobster Sam Giancana was shot and killed, while under FBI protective custody.

Mobster Johnny Roselli was killed shortly after he testified before the House Assassinations Committee in 1976.

George De Mohrenschildt, Oswald's Dallas handler, was killed hours before testifying to the House Committee in 1977.

William Sullivan, Hoover's number two man, who headed up the FBI investigation of the assassination of President Kennedy, was shot and killed in 1977, after completing a preliminary meeting with investigators for the House Select Committee on Assassinations.

Rep. Allard Lowenstein, Boggs' close collaborator, was shot and killed in 1980.

It Breaks Your Heart

Question: What are your thoughts for today's Congress?

Gallagher: I gave it a try. I gave it a try, and I smashed my whole career, as a result of it. And I'm not sorry! Because, what the hell would be the sense of staying down there, not being able to look in the mirror, or anything. And I think the overall picture, of the emerging of the secret-police apparatus in America, which really came to a head with the Kennedy assassination, is, today, bigger and stronger than ever. And you don't really have a Hoover around today, but you have a heck of a lot of guys with the power that Hoover had, who are a little more quiet and a little more efficient in the exercise of that kind of power. And I worry very much about what the hell's going to happen to this country, unless people become aware of it. The frailty of civilization, and the ability to destroy it is so widespread now. As long as people in the Congress don't raise these questions about the role of the secret govern-

LPACTV

Gallagher's 2003 biography, by Ron Felber, has been described by reviewers as timely, thoughtful, and perceptive—and a page-turner.

ment in America, or the secret *governments* in America, or the real role of the secret societies in America—as long as there's no protection for them, they can be destroyed overnight.

So, the power of destroying people is a lot easier even now than it was then. So, in answer to your question, there's a lot of courageous guys down there! I'm sure most of the people who get elected are well intentioned. We're all "Mr. Smith Goes to Washington"; you want to do the right thing. I'm speaking about the general people who seek election. They take all the fire you have to take to be in public life, you've got to have something other than collecting money, for fundraising or PACs. You want to make it a little better.

And you get down there, and you know, being a congressman or senator is one of the greatest jobs in the world! I mean, the pay is okay now. You're a celebrity, everybody's "Yes, Congressman. No, Congressman." And "Make way for the Congressman," and all of that, and that's great! Except, you come to a point, where now, you say: "Gee, I'm in this position, I've got what appears to be a lot of power—but I can't do anything about anything!"

Now, it breaks your heart.

It breaks your heart, since you see what has to be done, you're *close* enough to see what has to be done, what *should* be done, what Congress as a whole could do, but can't do any more.

I think the most important lesson is, if you have an issue that's worthwhile going to war about, you better damn well have an army behind you. I didn't.